ONE THING IS NECESSARY

ONE THING IS NECESSARY

THE WISDOM OF A CHRIST-CENTERED LIFE

BILL CROWDER

One Thing Is Necessary: The Wisdom of a Christ-Centered Life

Throughout, bold in Scripture quotations has been added by the author for emphasis.

Interior design by Michael J. Williams

Library of Congress Cataloging-in-Publication Data

Names: Crowder, Bill, author.
Title: One thing is necessary : the wisdom of a Christ-centered life / Bill Crowder.
Description: Grand Rapids, MI : Our Daily Bread Publishing, [2022] | Summary: "Witness the power and wisdom found in focusing on God and to live a Christ-centered life in a world full of distractions"-- Provided by publisher.
Identifiers: LCCN 2021049287 | ISBN 9781640701670
Subjects: LCSH: Christian life. | Distraction (Psychology)--Religious aspects--Christianity.
Classification: LCC BV4509.5 .C774 2022 | DDC 248.4--dc23/eng/20211118
LC record available at https://lccn.loc.gov/2021049287

Printed in the United States of America
22 23 24 25 26 26 28 29 / 8 7 6 5 4 3 2 1

To friends who opened doors for me for ministry:
Dave Randlett, Don Hescott, Ray Warren, and Bob Provost
Thanks.

CONTENTS

ACKNOWLEDGMENTS

For years, I have been a massive supporter of Liverpool Football Club, English Premier League champions for 2019–2020. In the world of football (what we Americans call soccer), there are two ways to build a team. One is to find a superstar of surpassing ability—a Lionel Messi or a Cristiano Ronaldo, for example—and then assemble the pieces and parts of the team to support that player's individual brilliance. Over the years, Real Madrid and Barcelona ruled the Spanish football league using that model.

Liverpool was built differently. While filled with world-class players, the Reds are about the collective rather than the individual. The group. The team. This is a very different model. It requires each player not only to fill his role but also to work together with others as they form a single unit to accomplish the team's goals. I love that. I love it because it is so much more sustainable, and I love it because it gives great value to every player on the team's roster. All have a role to play, and every member of the team is essential.

This is how our wise God builds the body of Christ—a group of gifted believers who depend on God and each other for the welfare of the body and the advance of the gospel. All of this is taught clearly in 1 Corinthians 12.

I would suggest that this is also the way a book like this is produced. The old adage says, "Many hands make light work," and that includes the work of book publishing. It is mind-boggling to think about how many hands are involved, and I am grateful for each hand that has carried some of the weight of this project. From Dave Branon, who polished and edited, to Peggy Willison, who proofread the text to comb any final errors from it. From Dawn Anderson, Ken Petersen, Chriscynethia Floyd, Joel Armstrong, and the Our Daily Bread Publishing team that helped to process the ideas and purify the concept, to Heather Brewer, Marjie Johnson, and Melissa Wade, who worked on designing and marketing the book so it could ultimately find its way into your hands. Like I said, it is about the collective—and I am privileged to work with the best.

Such a strong publishing team can only be surpassed by my personal home team. My wife, Marlene, has been my stalwart partner for over forty years, and she brings great wisdom and insight to what I do—including books like this one. Our kids (still numbering five) and grandkids (now numbering eight) are not only sources of great illustration material but also welcome cheerleaders when things drag on and are challenging. My mom was always my best reader, and I have always been grateful for her many years of wonderful support. She has recently gone to be with the Lord, but her wisdom and encouragement still echo lovingly in my heart. I am deeply thankful.

Ultimately, I am grateful to my heavenly Father, my

rescuing Savior, and the indwelling Spirit for allowing me to serve the body of Christ and to represent Jesus to the world. It is an unbelievable privilege for which I am grateful, and while the folks I have mentioned (and others I could have named) are vital in this work, it is my God who is the point of the work and the power behind it. He is the true and undisputed One Thing that gives life meaning and purpose and joy. As always, this is for Him.

INTRODUCTION

"THERE'S JUST ONE MORE THING"

The old TV detective show *Columbo* was unusual in the crime drama genre because each episode opened by showing the crime being committed. Therefore, everyone watching knew without a doubt who the guilty party was. The mystery of the program was in how the case would be solved and how the guilty person would be brought to justice for the crime.

Enter Lieutenant Columbo. The detective, played brilliantly by Peter Falk, would wander in wearing his rumpled overcoat and meander his way through the case until he thought he knew who the guilty person was. That began a kind of war of attrition in which Columbo would wear down his suspect. Every conversation would begin innocently, then, just as he turned to leave, Columbo would stop and say, "There's just one more thing," or, "Just one thing." Eventually the crime would be solved—but I was always struck by how often the determination to solve the mystery was fueled by Columbo's energetic pursuit of "just one thing."

One thing. It speaks of focus. It speaks of relentlessness. It speaks of a refusal to be distracted, which raises a terrifically important question:

What distracts you? What distracts me?

It could be hobbies or responsibilities. It could be relationships or religion. Which raises another question: Is distraction always a bad thing? Probably not, because we all know there are times of great stress and pressure when having a healthy distraction can provide a moment of profound relief.

I think we can also agree, however, that some distractions are negative or problematic. Studies show that the current trends toward multitasking, such as looking at multiple screens at the same time throughout a day, can be a source of real problems—problems like attention deficit disorder, where the ability to focus is marginalized by constant and diverse sources of nonstop input.

Additionally, there are many times when you don't want people to be distracted in any way because it can be genuinely dangerous. All of us feel a bit of concern when we watch people go flying past us on the highway at eighty miles an hour while texting, or doing their nails, or reading the newspaper, or eating a bowl of cereal (yes, I have personally witnessed all those things).

I think it's safe to assume that none of us would want our doctor to be distracted while performing surgery on us, or our pilot to be distracted while landing a jumbo jet. The examples could go on, but this should suffice to remind us how important focus is. And that takes us back to Lt. Columbo and his pursuit of "just one thing." He demonstrated a focus that borders on tenacity—and that should get our attention.

Focus matters.

That brings us to the subject of this book. Because we live in a world of distractions, the wisdom of the Scriptures reminds us that there are things—"one things"—that are worth focusing on. That are worth setting aside distractions for. That deserve our relentless attention. By focusing on the phrase "one thing," we find that the Bible reminds us that these critically important things deserve our undistracted focus.

I invite you to consider them together with me.

1

FOCUSING ON A MISSING THING

Looking at him, Jesus showed love to him and said to him, "*One thing* you lack."

Mark 10:21

During the long, cold, snowy Michigan winters, Marlene and I often worked jigsaw puzzles to keep our brains active when we couldn't get outside to stay active physically. We worked all different kinds of puzzles, from landscapes to cityscapes to album covers to sports stadiums to world maps to, well, you name it. One of my favorite puzzles was a nostalgia piece called (yes, puzzles do sometimes have names) "Things I Ate as a Kid." It was a crazy quilt of the labels and packaging of all kinds of old-school snacks and sweets—many of which, in fact, I did eat as a child.

When we completed a puzzle we were particularly fond of

(several puzzles depicting the major sites of London come to mind), Marlene would glue it together, frame it, and hang it on the wall. As a result, in my man cave the walls were covered with framed puzzles that actually made for an interesting form of art that I really enjoyed. Except for one puzzle.

This particular puzzle had rich colors and an interesting image. It filled a nice spot on the wall.

But it had one piece missing.

One piece.

Where did it go? Obviously, we don't know—but I am a bit suspicious. When one of our grandsons was younger and a puzzle was being worked on anywhere around him, he would often hide one piece so he could have the honor of putting the final piece of the puzzle into place. I wonder if little Nathan hid this piece and forgot where he'd put it. But after weeks of searching and not finding it, Marlene decided to glue and frame the puzzle anyway.

Every time I looked at that puzzle, my eyes were immediately drawn to the one solitary open space. It would never be quite right because something was missing.

At a more important level, missing things can be disturbing—like a missing pet that creates a vacuum in a family.

Missing things can be infuriating—like a pass interference call that seems obvious but goes uncalled, costing a team a trip to the Super Bowl. New Orleans Saints fans know what that's all about.

Missing things can be confusing—like a piece of information that, if known, could alter our perspective about something. Or someone.

Missing things matter.

In one of Jesus's most memorable encounters with a

citizen of Judea, there are many things that are good. There are many things that are right. There are many things that are notable.

But the story rises and falls on one thing—a missing thing—and it is on that one thing that Jesus focuses His attention and concern.

The Right Question

In a world filled with so-called experts who seemingly have all the answers, there is much to be said for asking the right questions. This truth has not gone unnoticed:

> "Ask the right questions if you're going to find the right answers." —Vanessa Redgrave

> "Asking the right questions takes as much skill as giving the right answers." —Robert Half

> "The uncreative mind can spot wrong answers, but it takes a very creative mind to spot wrong questions." —Antony Jay

This certainly applies in matters of faith. Some of the greatest philosophical questions of life scream out all around us, and they are good questions.

- *Where did we come from?* This question explores our point of origin, and it is significant, at least in part, because it can help to define our value as human beings—or our relative lack of value. Point of origin is a big deal.
- *Why am I here?* None of us want to feel that our lives are without purpose. We don't want to think that we are

simply taking up space or getting in the way of everyone else. A sense of purpose is core to a meaningful life.

- *What happens after death?* The mystery of what takes place (as Pastor Erwin Lutzer put it) "one minute after you die" speaks to the question of our mortality. If all of life is in the here and now, we would be driven to make very different kinds of decisions than if we believe that there is a life beyond this life. A life beyond the grave.
- *Where can I find hope?* The year 2020 was marked by a global pandemic, social unrest, and (at least in the United States) some of the most disheartening and divisive political campaigning we have ever seen. These and hundreds of other personal experiences created an atmosphere of hopelessness that was deeply discouraging. Finding hope is critical to navigating the traumas and turbulence of life.

In Jesus's day, people also wrestled with a number of significant questions, some of them related to questions we continue to struggle with in our day. But one question rose above the rest. It was the question that was debated in synagogues and yeshivas. It was a question rabbis focused on because of its obvious significance—and it's the question that is brought to Jesus in Mark 10.

> As [Jesus] was setting out on a journey, a man ran up to Him and knelt before Him, and asked Him, "Good Teacher, what shall I do so that I may inherit eternal life?" (v. 17)

Mark's gospel has sometimes been referred to by scholars as a passion narrative with an extended introduction.

They say that because more than a third of the book (chapters 11–16) covers the events of Jesus's final incarnate week on earth. This makes the timing for this question critical. Jesus is making His way to Jerusalem where He will ultimately experience the cross and resurrection (the key events of that passion narrative). These are events Jesus will predict for the third time directly following His encounter with this man and his question (vv. 32–34). In fact, the very next chapter (Mark 11) opens with Jesus's triumphal entry into Jerusalem—the scene that sets the events of His crucifixion in motion. As we look back at this from our perspective, we discover that the timing matters because the events of the Passover week are anticipated in the very question that is brought to Jesus. At Passover, the Jewish people celebrated their rescue from bondage and slavery in Egypt with a sacrificial lamb, perfectly setting the stage for Jesus—the Lamb of God—to rescue people from slavery and bondage to sin so they might inherit eternal life through His own sacrifice on the cross.

It is in this time, as the cross is nearing, that a man with a question approaches Jesus. The man is commonly remembered as the "rich young ruler," a title that only comes together when you combine the way he is described in the three synoptic gospel accounts. We find here in Mark that the man is rich; "he had great wealth" (v. 22 NIV). In Luke 18:18, we are told that this man was a ruler (Greek *archon*), referring to someone serving in a public office. Matthew adds that he was young (19:22). Hence, "rich young ruler."

Earlier, we mentioned that in this encounter there are many good things. Many right things. We see some of those good things here at the outset by examining the manner of the young man's approach to the Teacher from Nazareth. Notice the following:

- *He came running* . . . no doubt excited, perhaps even desperate, to hear Jesus's answer to the question that weighed on his heart. This young man had probably heard the answers of any number of other rabbis, yet he remained unsatisfied. He approached the Messiah with anxious anticipation that perhaps Jesus could provide clarity regarding this much-debated issue.
- *He came with humility* . . . kneeling before Jesus—a position that must have shocked those observing the meeting. People of status and position in the ancient world were expected to conduct themselves with a certain kind of decorum. To see a ruler (even a young one) kneeling before anyone, let alone an itinerant rabbi, would have bordered on the scandalous.
- *He came to the right person* . . . with his question. We cannot know with certainty to what degree the young man was aware of Jesus's unique qualifications to answer a question regarding the eternal, but for us, who recognize Jesus as the eternal Son of God, it is clear that the young man could have found no better source for help in this matter.
- *He came with the right question* . . . the question of eternal life. By definition, this is an all-important question. Remember our earlier consideration of the importance of asking the right questions (see page 19). There can be no doubt that the rich young ruler is spot on with the legitimacy of his concern about the issue of eternity.

You have to be somewhat taken by this young man. There is so much good here! At first glance, you would have to think that this rich young ruler is in the right place to find answers. Beyond that, he is also in exactly the right place *spiritually* to meet the Messiah, who alone can give eternal life (see John 20:30–31)—let alone answer questions about it.

But while everything the young man does seems good and right, making great sense, it is the initial reaction of Jesus to him that causes us to scratch our heads.

An Unexpected Response

One of the most famous pieces of music over the last fifty-some years is Don McLean's brilliant "American Pie." Lamenting the deaths of musicians Buddy Holly, The Big Bopper (J. P. Richardson), and Ritchie Valens in the crash of a small plane in 1959, McLean gives a musical history of rock and roll using symbolism and word pictures that have had musicologists scrutinizing them for their meaning for the last five decades. Viewed by some as a musical masterpiece, by others as an enigma, and by still others as one of pop music's enduring standards, "American Pie" has caused unending speculation as to the explanation of all those word pictures as people try to discern what it all means.

The response of the song's author and singer, however, is surprising. When asked what "American Pie" means, McLean simply replied (no doubt tongue in cheek), "It means I don't ever have to work again if I don't want to."

When I first read that response, I have to admit I was shocked. It certainly wasn't what I expected!

In an eternally more important matter, when the rich

young man approached Jesus with the question of eternity, Jesus responded with an even more mystifying response that took the form of a pair of responses mashed together:

> But Jesus said to him, "Why do you call Me good? No one is good except God alone. You know the commandments: 'Do not murder, Do not commit adultery, Do not steal, Do not give false witness, Do not defraud, Honor your father and mother.'" (Mark 10:18–19)

An unexpected question about goodness. Jesus begins by questioning the questioner about the question itself! "Why do you call Me good?" is a challenge to the man's presuppositions. In Romans 3:12, Paul would later write, "There is no one who does good, there is not even one," paraphrasing Ecclesiastes 7:20. So, what is Jesus saying to the rich young ruler? Is He denying His goodness—a vital character quality of the God we encounter in the Scriptures? Certainly not.

What may be in play here is that since only God could be viewed as truly and essentially good, by ascribing goodness to Jesus the young man was making a statement that he may or may not have fully understood or intended. What may have been intended as a simple compliment was unacceptable because it may have sounded like empty flattery. In essence, Jesus could be challenging him to be careful how he uses words. Words have meanings and those meanings matter. Jesus is not denying either His deity or His essential goodness, but He is underlining to the young man the importance of both understanding and meaning what he says.

An unexpected citation of the law. As people living on this side of the cross and resurrection, hearing Jesus answer the man's question about eternal life by reciting the Ten Commandments knocks us off-balance. As we examine the teachings of the New Testament, we see overwhelming evidence that eternal life is a result of grace, not law. In fact, in John's prologue to his gospel, we read that "the Law was given through Moses; grace and truth were realized through Jesus Christ" (1:17). Yet Jesus lists the Commandments of Moses rather than highlighting the grace His coming cross would furnish.

Commentators regularly point out that what Jesus lists are, arguably, the easier elements of the Commandments. The first portion of the Ten Commandments is vertical, pointing to our relationship with God, while those listed here by Jesus are horizontal and deal with human relationships.

Why does this matter? Because, again, asking the right question matters. The issue is in the nature of the question itself. By saying "What shall I do . . . ?" (Mark 10:17), the rich young man's assumption is that eternal life is something to be achieved—as opposed to eternal life being a gift that is received. In response, Jesus does not affirm that keeping the law is the key to achieving eternal life. He responds to the man's presupposition by listing the very kind of things the young man apparently thought would meet the requirements. I would suggest that Jesus's words "You know the commandments" (v. 19) are not an endorsement of performance-oriented salvation but an attempt to make the young man carry his assumptions to their logical conclusion.

A response that may be shocking to us would no doubt have caused the rich young ruler to nod his head and think, Okay, that's what I thought. Why can we assume that to be his reaction? Notice how the young man responds to Jesus's listing of the law.

A Poignant Interaction

Misunderstanding is a dangerous thing—especially when we misunderstand people's hearts and intents. Although understanding the rich young ruler's heart may seem straightforward, it would be very easy for us to misunderstand this young man. Thankfully, Jesus was in no such danger of misunderstanding, as we see in His response to the young man's honest answer to Jesus's statement:

> And he said to Him, "Teacher, I have kept all these things from my youth." Looking at him, Jesus showed love to him and said to him, "**One thing** you lack: go and sell all you possess and give to the poor, and you will have treasure in heaven; and come, follow Me." (vv. 20–21)

I must confess that when I read the young man's words, "Teacher, I have kept all these things from my youth," I experience some fairly unpleasant reactions. After all, no one is capable of keeping the law. Peter made that clear when arguing against holding non-Jewish Christians to Moses's law, saying, "Why are you putting God to the test by placing upon the neck of the disciples a yoke which neither our forefathers nor we have been able to bear?" (Acts 15:10). In spite of that reality, I hear the young man's claim and the mental image of the Pharisee comes into my mind, and in those words I hear religious arrogance. I hear self-righteousness. I hear self-satisfaction. I hear smugness.

And I am dead wrong.

How do I know that I am so far off base?

Because Jesus's response to the young man's words is categorically different from my response. Jesus doesn't hear what I hear because Jesus has access to information I don't have. As we read in the Old Testament, "Man looks at the outward appearance, but the LORD looks at the heart" (1 Samuel 16:7).

This was not exclusively a characteristic of Old Testament Jehovah either.

In the New Testament gospel of John, we find the critically important encounter between Jesus, the Teacher from Nazareth, and Nicodemus, the teacher of Israel. Unfortunately, however, we naturally begin reading the account at John 3:1. The out-of-place chapter division (added centuries later by scholars) robs us of the necessary introduction to the meeting between these two teachers, for that introduction is found at the conclusion of John 2:

> But Jesus, on His part, was not entrusting Himself to them, because He knew all people, and because He did not need anyone to testify about mankind, for He Himself knew what was in mankind. (vv. 24–25)

Jesus knew what was in the mind of Nicodemus, and He knew what was in the heart and mind of this young man as well. That is why He reacts so differently from how I would naturally respond. He knows. Mark 10:21 gives us that response: "Then Jesus, looking at him, loved him" (NKJV).

Don't run past that idea too quickly. Sit with it.

Focus on the wonder of Jesus loving him. Why?

Because this language is far rarer in the Gospels than you might think. Therefore, it may be intended to get our attention.

Where do we find statements of Jesus specifically loving individuals? Oddly enough, aside from this event in Mark 10, all other such statements are concentrated in the gospel of John, where Jesus loves these individuals:

- The disciples in general (13:1)
- John, the disciple Jesus loved, in particular (e.g., 13:23)
- Martha and Mary, the sisters of Lazarus (11:5)
- Lazarus (11:3, 36)

That is amazing! While we know through the cross the depths of the love of Christ for us—and for all—the language of that love is most uncommon in the Gospels. The narrator of Mark 10 doesn't tell us specifically what prompted Jesus's response of love for the rich young ruler, but I think it is eminently clear. Jesus saw in that young man's heart the very opposite of what I supposed. Where I saw arrogance, Jesus saw authenticity. Where I saw self-righteousness, Jesus saw genuine attempts at faithfulness.

Looking into the heart of this rich young ruler, Jesus saw many wonderful things, prompting a response of love for the man kneeling at His feet.

Yet, amid the many wonderful things Jesus saw in this heart, there was a missing thing. Now we come to our key phrase, "one thing." It is the missing puzzle piece. That one bit that brings the entire picture together with perfect clarity and completion.

Seeing what's missing demands extraordinarily clear sight.

And what Jesus sees provokes yet another surprising response from Him:

> **One thing** you lack: go and sell all you possess and give to the poor, and you will have treasure in heaven; and come, follow Me. (v. 21)

How are we to understand that? There is no way Jesus is teaching salvation by means of philanthropy. Remember what we saw when Jesus recited the law to the young man. We have the benefit of the post-resurrection understanding that salvation is of grace, not works, for we have Scripture that the rich young ruler did not:

> For by grace you have been saved through faith; and this is not of yourselves, it is the gift of God; not a result of works, so that no one may boast. (Ephesians 2:8–9)

So then, what are we to make of Jesus's words? I would suggest that, as before, Jesus is speaking into the young man's context—and showing him that, in fact, he has *not* kept all these things from his youth.

Why can we say that? Because the young man was missing the point of the law. In another conversation with another questioner, Jesus expressed the greatest commandment this way:

> Jesus answered, "The foremost is, 'Hear, Israel! The Lord is our God, the Lord is one; and you shall love the Lord your God with all your heart, and with all your soul, and with all your mind, and with all your strength.' The second is this: 'You shall love your neighbor as yourself.' There is no other commandment greater than these." (Mark 12:29–31)

The apostle Paul drove the point home even further:

> For the whole Law is fulfilled in one word, in the statement, "You shall love your neighbor as yourself." (Galatians 5:14)

When Jesus challenged the rich young ruler with the horizontal relational elements of the law, he answered with confidence that he had passed the test. But Jesus says that for all his good deeds, the young man is missing the one thing that would truly display the kind of obedience he is claiming—the love that flows out of love for the Father.

Jesus looked at him and loved him, but how does the young man respond to that love? "But he was deeply dismayed by these words, and he went away grieving; for he was one who owned much property" (Mark 10:22).

This is the key. He owned much but was unwilling to part with it, even though that parting would put on display the kind of love that is the entire summation of the law the young man claimed to have fulfilled.

The nature of this sad conclusion becomes even clearer when we see the account of the rich young ruler in Luke's gospel. Luke gives us this encounter in 18:18–23—positioning the rich young ruler as the perfect setup for what follows.

What follows in Luke 19 is the story of another rich man, Zaccheus the chief tax collector. Whereas the rich young man went away saddened by Jesus's suggestion that he give away his wealth in order to love his neighbor, Zaccheus needs no such suggestion.

He volunteers!

Upon encountering the Christ, Zaccheus, who had become enormously wealthy by defrauding his Jewish neighbors through collecting taxes for their Roman conquerors, automatically declares:

> Behold, Lord, half of my possessions I am giving to the poor, and if I have extorted anything from anyone, I am giving back four times as much. (v. 8)

What the rich young ruler withheld, Zaccheus freely offered. Not as an act to earn the eternal life the young man sought but as evidence that he had already received it. This we know because of what followed in Zaccheus's story:

> And Jesus said to him, "Today salvation has come to this house, because he, too, is a son of Abraham. For the Son of Man has come to seek and to save that which was lost." (vv. 9–10)

"Salvation has come" is the answer to the question "What shall I do so that I may inherit eternal life?" Salvation came to Zaccheus because he responded to Jesus the Savior, and the evidence was this: for the first time in his adult life, Zaccheus was loving his neighbor as himself. The question is not "What shall I do?" but rather, "What will reveal that I *have* received eternal life?" Zaccheus's love for others was the inevitable by-product of having received the love of Jesus.

John draws his gospel account to a close by explaining why he wrote it:

> These have been written so that you may believe that Jesus is the Christ, the Son of God; and that by believing you may have life in His name. (20:31)

The rich young ruler did not embrace the clearly stated love of Christ, and the evidence was seen as he sadly walked away—clutching his possessions and missing the love of Christ that alone brings the life he was searching for. He missed the one thing that would reveal the fruit of a changed heart.

Again, as people of the cross and the empty tomb, we clearly have access to information that the rich young ruler didn't have. But in a very different way, he had direct personal access to Jesus and His love in a way we don't physically have. Ultimately, the issue is nothing less than this:

How will I respond to the love of
Christ that brings eternal life?

George Cooper and Ira Sankey's wonderful hymn frames the heart that embraces that love and is changed by it to love others as well:

There are lonely hearts to cherish,
While the days are going by;
There are weary souls who perish,
While the days are going by;
If a smile we can renew,
As our journey we pursue,
Oh, the good we all may do,
While the days are going by.

While the days are going by;
Let your face be like the morning,

While the days are going by;
Oh, the world is full of sighs,
Full of sad and weeping eyes;
Help your fallen brother rise,
While the days are going by.

Questions for Personal Reflection or Group Discussion

1. What are some missing things that have caused you concern or grief or heartache? What made their absence so difficult?
2. What about the young man's behavior do you find most surprising? In what ways was his behavior wonderful? In what ways was it disappointing?
3. Ponder the statement that "Jesus, looking at him, loved him." What is more surprising, that Jesus felt love for someone who seems spiritually out of step, or that the language of Jesus's love for specific individuals is so rare in the Gospels? Why?
4. Why did the young man's determination to cling to his possessions reflect a wrong heart? In our culture, why might we struggle with the command Jesus gave him?
5. Consider the contrasting descriptions of the rich young ruler (Mark 10) and Zaccheus the tax collector (Luke 19). Which do you most readily identify with? Why?

2

FOCUSING ON AN EXPERIENCED THING

He then answered, "Whether He is a sinner, I do not know; ***one thing*** I do know, that though I was blind, now I see."

John 9:25

As a lifelong fan of the Cleveland Browns in the National Football League, the past couple of decades have been frustrating as the revolving door of general managers, head coaches, and quarterbacks have made the franchise a target for the jokes and mockery of the media, fans of other teams, and even Browns fans themselves. In fact, Browns fans at one time began calling the Browns' home stadium the "Factory of Sadness." Such is the level of despair among fans of one of the more storied franchises in NFL history.

As I write this in early 2020, an all-too-familiar cycle repeated itself as the Browns once again fired their head coach and hired a new one. The selection raised more than a few eyebrows. Why? Because the team's hierarchy had once again selected a head coach with no head-coaching experience. Now, to be sure, that does not mean that the new coach was unqualified—but fans wondered if perhaps he was simply underqualified. Replacing a head coach who had no previous head-coaching experience with another head coach with no previous head-coaching experience could neatly fit into what is often called the definition of *insanity*: doing the same thing in the same way over and over again while expecting different results.

Now, this is not a rant against the Browns; I remain a loyal though weary fan. Nor is it a knock on the newly hired coach. Clearly to get to that level in any endeavor requires a great deal of work, and admittedly head-coaching experience does not guarantee a trip to the Super Bowl. My point is that there are few things in life more valuable than experience. Whether you're evaluating pastoral candidates, political candidates, job candidates, or even head-coaching candidates, there is no substitute for experience.

Perhaps that is why someone has said, "Good decisions are the fruit of experience, and experience is the fruit of bad decisions." We learn by learning—and part of learning is coming to grips with the reality of the things we learn in the living of life. It's tutelage in the school of experience—touted by Julius Caesar as the "teacher of all things."

While learning experiences are often challenging, sometimes painful, and occasionally brutal, they also tend to be unforgettable. Experience marks us—sometimes for good and sometimes for ill. But it marks us nonetheless. And in some ways, experience *makes* us.

As a result, experience is not to be taken lightly. It needs to be taken seriously. And when one particular experience has been the defining reality of your life for decades, it needs to be understood.

Such is the case with the man we encounter in this chapter.

He is a man defined by his dominant life experience—an experience he neither asked for nor caused.

He was born blind.

Jesus and the Blind

In recent years, we have seen wave after wave of viruses, diseases, and pandemics, from HIV to SARS to H1N1 to COVID-19. It seems that we are in a constant state of anticipation (or anxiety) about the next sweeping condition that will impact people all around us—maybe even impacting us as well.

Such was the pervasiveness of blindness in the first century. Blindness was seemingly everywhere in the days of Jesus, in part because personal hygiene was not consistently practiced. *The International Standard Bible Encyclopedia* says that there are fifty-four references to blindness in the Scriptures, often caused by disease:

> The commonest disease is a purulent ophthalmia, a highly infectious condition propagated largely by the flies which can be seen infesting the crusts of dried secretion undisturbed

> even on the eyes of infants. . . . This almost always leaves the eyes damaged with bleared lids, opacities of the cornea, and sometimes extensive internal injury as well.

With blindness existing at such a ubiquitous level, it comes as no surprise that Jesus encountered it on such a regular basis. Yet, while His meetings with the visually impaired were frequent, they were not random or without purpose. Jesus's healing of blind people was intended to be seen as evidence of His messianic identity. When He inaugurated His public ministry at the synagogue of Nazareth, Jesus claimed Isaiah's messianic prophecy as He read from the sacred scrolls:

> The Spirit of the Lord is upon Me,
> Because He anointed Me to bring good news
> to the poor.
> He has sent Me to proclaim release to captives,
> And recovery of sight to the blind,
> To set free those who are oppressed."
> (Luke 4:18)

Clearly, the messianic prophecies of the Old Testament were intended to prepare the people of Israel to recognize the Messiah when He arrived. And part of the messianic mission was to be validated and evidenced in bringing sight to the blind.

At one point, when he was imprisoned and in despair, John the Baptist sent his disciples to Jesus to ask if indeed Jesus was the Christ (from *christos*, the Greek equivalent of the Hebrew word *messiah*, meaning "anointed one"). Matthew recorded Jesus's response as one that drew from those messianic prophecies.

> Jesus answered and said to them, "Go and report to John what you hear and see: those who are blind receive sight and those who limp walk, those with leprosy are cleansed and those who are deaf hear, the dead are raised, and the poor have the gospel preached to them. And blessed is any person who does not take offense at Me." (11:4–6)

"The blind receive sight" was the link connecting Jesus's identity to the prophecy of Isaiah (see Isaiah 42:7). When the Messiah came, there would be verifiable evidence that all could see—even the blind.

So Jesus was continually confronted with the blind—and the Gospels provide us with repeated accounts of the Master healing those who were blind. From the blind man at Bethsaida (Mark 8:22–26) to blind Bartimaeus in Jericho (Luke 18:35–43), the blind had their sight restored. Sometimes with a word, sometimes with a touch, and sometimes with spittle, Jesus healed the blind in a variety of ways—but heal them He did.

Each of the many cases of blindness in the Gospels is remarkable, and no doubt each of the healed persons celebrated with great delight at having their sight restored. But with all the healings Jesus performed for blind individuals, one rises above the rest—because, though many are described in the Gospels as being blind, only this man is described as having been *born* blind.

The Blind Man's Experience

One of the great realities of life in ancient Israel (as well as life in the Middle East today) is that it was dominated by the collective as opposed to the individual. Individual lives found value and worth within the larger context of relationship—first within the family and then within the village or neighborhood, then within the religious community. This is a bit challenging for those of us in the West, where individualism rules. We find worth and value in ourselves and what we accomplish on a personal level, but that is not the case in a collective environment. It is not about *me*; it is about the *group*. The community is all.

That is why, as we approach the story of the man born blind, we can't simply consider his personal experience. It is very important that we understand how his community experienced his blindness with him. John 9 opens with Jesus and His disciples leaving the temple compound in Jerusalem, where they encounter this blind man begging at the temple gate. While it sounds strange to us, this was actually a service that disabled people provided to the community. One of the basic tenets of Judaism was giving alms to the poor, so not only did begging provide a meager livelihood for the beggar but it also provided an opportunity to fulfill a religious obligation for those coming to the temple for worship. As we will see, this man is a fixture at the temple and is well-known for his continual begging there.

When the disciples ask Jesus a theological question about the man, Jesus responds that the affliction the man has suffered was not the result of a particular sin by himself or his parents, but it was intended for God's glory. Then He says:

> "While I am in the world, I am the Light of the world." When He had said this, He spit on the ground, and made

> mud from the saliva, and applied the mud to his eyes, and said to him, "Go, wash in the pool of Siloam" (which is translated, Sent). So he left and washed, and came back seeing. (vv. 5–7)

He "came back seeing." Extraordinary. Imagine the wonder this man feels as he for the first time sees the beauty of a blue sky. Or the magnificence of the Jerusalem temple. Or the intricacies of an almond tree in bloom. The level of information overload in his first sighted moments must have been overwhelming.

This man who was born into darkness and experienced nothing but darkness his entire life now experiences light in his world because he has encountered the Light of the World. But remember—this is not simply about the man and his miraculous healing. His personal experience of darkness has been lived out in the larger community, and *his* experience has also been part of *their* experience. That is why John tells us not only how Jesus impacted the man by giving him his sight but also how the collective responded to this most unexpected of situations.

The Neighbors. For the neighbors, the experience was one of confusion. And rightly so. They had shared a community with the man and his family. They knew him and knew him well. Imagine living in the same neighborhood with someone who has been blind from birth—only to see him fully healed and able to function in a sighted world. John records their response:

> So the neighbors, and those who previously saw him as a beggar, were saying, "Is this not the one who used to sit and

> beg?" Others were saying, "This is he," still others were saying, "No, but he is like him." The man himself kept saying, "I am the one." (vv. 8–9)

As you picture the confusion of the neighbors, try to imagine the frustration of the formerly blind man. Because his healing defies human explanation, some of his neighbors assume he isn't even the same man! The irony here is that they have seen him his entire life, yet they aren't sure they know him. He is seeing for the first time, and he has no doubt that he knows them! He affirms that, in fact, he is the same man, and when they ask how he can now see, he explains the change in his life simply:

> The man who is called Jesus made mud, and spread it on my eyes, and said to me, "Go to Siloam and wash"; so I went away and washed, and I received sight. (v. 11)

Whether or not they accept the explanation the man gives, one thing is certain. In the eyes of the community, this entire matter is a mystery. A confusing mystery.

The religious community. For the religious establishment, this event is both a nightmare and a kind of tipping point—in part because of the impact it has on the community. While some forms of sight deficiency could, in theory at least, be treated with salves and medicines, someone with congenital blindness was hopeless. Yet, as we have seen, this blind man "came back seeing." For the religious leaders this creates a situation that must be neutralized, yet how do they neutralize Jesus, who has done such a matchless miracle?

For some time now in the gospel of John, the religionists

have been trying to dismantle Jesus's credibility. Now they have this to deal with, so they challenge the legitimacy of the man's experience, hoping that by destroying the formerly blind man's credibility they can also undermine Jesus's credibility.

> They brought the man who was previously blind to the Pharisees. Now it was a Sabbath on the day that Jesus made the mud and opened his eyes. Then the Pharisees also were asking him again how he received his sight. And he said to them, "He applied mud to my eyes, and I washed, and I see." Therefore some of the Pharisees were saying, "This man is not from God, because He does not keep the Sabbath." But others were saying, "How can a man who is a sinner perform such signs?" And there was dissension among them. So they said again to the man who was blind, "What do you say about Him, since He opened your eyes?" And he said, "He is a prophet." (vv. 13–17)

This just won't do. For the religious leaders, the last thing they need is another messianic figure stirring up trouble and bringing down the wrath of Rome upon the nation. In early first-century Israel, a variety of people were put forth as potential candidates for the title of Messiah. Perhaps most notable among these individuals was Judas of Galilee, who led an anti-tax rebellion against the Roman occupiers—causing significant problems for those trying to maintain the very fragile applecart of coexistence between the nation of Israel and their Roman conquerors.

The man's parents. Now we turn to the more personal part of the community: the man's parents. If the neighbors were confused, the parents are dumbfounded. But now, in a sense, they take the witness stand to speak about the situation.

> The Jews then did not believe it about him, that he had been blind and had received sight, until they called the parents of the very one who had received his sight, and they questioned them, saying, "Is this your son, who you say was born blind? Then how does he now see?" His parents then answered and said, "We know that this is our son, and that he was born blind; but how he now sees, we do not know; or who opened his eyes, we do not know. Ask him; he is of age, he will speak for himself." His parents said this because they were afraid of the Jews; for the Jews had already reached the decision that if anyone confessed Him to be Christ, he was to be excommunicated from the synagogue. It was for this reason that his parents said, "He is of age; ask him." (vv. 18–23)

The parents are terrified that they will be excommunicated from the synagogue. Why? Again, it is because the collective was everything. Being cast out of the synagogue would effectively remove them from community life and, with it, the relationships necessary for work, worship, and welfare. They affirm their son's lifelong condition of blindness, but they cannot speak to the specifics of his current experience.

The neighbors struggle with a mystery.

The religious leaders seek to neutralize a problem.

The parents live in terror of being driven from the synagogue and community life.

The formerly blind man is left to speak for himself.

The Value of Experience

One day, I was stopped in the lunchroom at Our Daily Bread Ministries by a coworker with a question. This person wanted to know if I agreed with a statement her pastor had made the previous Sunday. "He said that all a person needed to know in order to be saved was that Christ rose from the dead, quoting, 'That if you confess with your mouth Jesus as Lord, and believe in your heart that God raised Him from the dead, you will be saved' [Romans 10:9]. Is that really all you need to know?"

I understand the question. But I also understand that we live in a culture that is driven by information. We have access to volumes of information that would have been unimaginable fifty years ago, much less two thousand years ago. As a result, we tend to informationalize everything—looking for an irreducible minimum of what must be known in order for virtually anything to occur. And that is how the reality of a courtroom or a university testing center or a ministerial ordination council becomes the grid through which we process much of life.

But that is today—a twenty-first century in which we are drowning in a tsunami of information.

What about in the first century?

I recently read a book about the four gospels in which the authors made a great deal out of the question, What if this gospel were the only one we had? If the gospel of Mark were our only witness of Christ, we would probably not celebrate Christmas because Mark gives no information of that event. We would not recite the Lord's Prayer. We would not reflect on the Beatitudes.

Why does this matter? Because in the first century, there were groups of believers that only had Mark's gospel. Compared to us, their information was severely limited—but, though limited, their information was more than adequate for them to make a faith decision. They were not equipped to answer every question of theology or practice—but they had the gospel.

That brings us back to our newly healed blind man. He was not equipped with the background or training to debate with the religious intelligentsia. He lacked the information for that heady exercise.

What he lacked in education and information, however, the formerly blind man more than made up for with experience, as we see in this passage from John's gospel:

> So for a second time they summoned the man who had been blind, and said to him, "Give glory to God; we know that this man is a sinner." He then answered, "Whether He is a sinner, I do not know; **one thing** I do know, that though I was blind, now I see." (9:24–25)

Years ago, I heard a speaker say that "a person with an experience is never at the mercy of a person with an argument." I'll confess that I was somewhat troubled at that, because experiences—like emotions—can be misleading. Experiences must be tested, and they must be tested against the Scriptures to ascertain their legitimacy.

Nevertheless, the fact that I may not be able to fully explain an experience does not in itself nullify its validity. As we have seen, had the religious leaders tested the man's experience against their own Scriptures, they would have found Isaiah and a host of other prophetic writings pointing to the healing of the blind as a promised reality in the long-anticipated age of the Messiah's coming. Tragically, instead of approaching the Scriptures, they attack the man.

Here is where the ex-blind man's genuine experience trumps his lack of information. He knows he is punching way above his weight class with these religious heavyweights. He knows he can't go toe-to-toe with them intellectually or informationally. What he can do, however, is reaffirm the genuineness of his experience.

When the religious leaders question Jesus's purity and character, the healed man hasn't the background or training to analyze the theology of the thing. Instead, in one of the most profound faith statements in the Bible, the man born blind simply restates his experience with Jesus:

> Whether He is a sinner, I do not know; **one thing** I do know, that though I was blind, now I see. (v. 25)

One thing. An experienced thing. A life that had been dominated in its entirety by the experience of blindness has now been transformed by the experience of sight and light.

He doesn't know about Jesus's background.

He doesn't know about Jesus's nature.

He doesn't know about Jesus's messianic office.

He *does* know one thing—Jesus has healed his blindness, and that is beyond dispute. That cannot be undone or ignored. It is the experiential answer to their theological queries. He doesn't know many things; he knows one thing. He knows the transformation of his entire life experience.

Jesus has made him whole.

What do you know? How does that knowledge position you to engage a life for which we often feel under equipped?

- Abraham knew that God had promised him a home and a lineage.
- Hagar knew that God both saw and heard her as she sought to carve out a life for herself and her son, Ishmael, in the wilderness.
- Joseph knew that God had promised him a role of leadership.
- Moses knew that God promised to go with him as he returned to Egypt.
- Ruth knew that Naomi's God was worthy of her attention and trust.
- David knew that a lion and a bear had prepared him for Goliath.
- Elijah knew that, at the right time, God would restore the rains.

They didn't know everything, but they knew enough—because they had seen their knowledge proven by God's faithfulness.

Often we feel underprepared to share our faith with those who don't know Jesus. We feel intimidated by not having the answers to every question. By not understanding the theological rationale for every argument.

But that misses the point. One of my Bible college profs said, "Sharing your faith is simply one beggar telling another beggar where they found bread." It isn't about having all the answers; it is about a relationship with the life-changing Christ.

I experienced this myself as I returned to my hometown to plant a church after several years of teaching at the Bible college I had previously attended. When I encountered people I had gone to school with (or the parents of girls I had dated), there were odd looks, challenging questions, and sometimes downright disbelief.

But I could look back and see the evidence of God's changing power. I could see the ways that I had once been blind. I knew the moment that He had made my spiritual blindness a thing of the past. For all my shortcomings, I knew what I had experienced through trusting in Him and His love.

I didn't need to dot every i or cross every t of theological nuance. I just needed to tell what Jesus had done for me. And that is still the best way to bear witness to Jesus. As someone has said, "I'm not what I ought to be and I'm not what I want to be—but thank God I'm not what I was."

One thing I know: once I was "blind," but now I see. Perhaps Katherine Hankey felt the same way, prompting her to write this beautiful hymn:

> I love to tell the story
> Of unseen things above,
> Of Jesus and His glory,
> Of Jesus and His love.
>
> I love to tell the story
> Because I know 'tis true;
> It satisfies my longings
> As nothing else can do.

I love to tell the story;
'Twill be my theme in glory
To tell the old, old story
Of Jesus and His love.

Questions for Personal Reflection or Group Discussion

1. What are some life experiences from which you have learned profound lessons? Were they good or bad experiences? What made them so instructive?
2. If you live in a Western culture, how does that lifetime of experience make it hard to really understand a culture where the community dominates and the individual is sublimated? If you live in an Eastern culture, how have you experienced the good and bad of the power of the collective?
3. Consider your own experience with Christ. What characterized the spiritual blindness you knew before you came to the Savior? How has your experience with Jesus changed your life, perspective, or attitudes?
4. Recognizing that bearing witness to Christ does not require a seminary education or absolute knowledge of every theological issue, write out your faith story and how you could share your experience with someone who doesn't yet know Jesus.
5. Pray for opportunities to share your story with someone who needs Christ.

3

FOCUSING ON A PURSUED THING

Brothers and sisters, I do not regard myself as having taken hold of it yet; but ***one thing*** I do: forgetting what lies behind and reaching forward to what lies ahead, I press on toward the goal for the prize of the upward call of God in Christ Jesus.

Philippians 3:13–14

A recent ad for a carmaker described its organizational ethos by saying that the company was about "the pursuit of perfection." *Pursuit* is an interesting word. It is a word heavily weighted with passion, commitment, and relentlessness. We might dabble in hobbies, dip our toe in the waters of activities, or try on for size some novel new thing—but what we pursue speaks deeply into what we feel we are all about. It's something like . . .

- The athletes who, with all that is in them, pursue a hallowed record in their chosen sport, like Henry Aaron breaking Babe Ruth's career home run mark.
- The research scientist who, through long hours and endless experimentation, pursues a cure for a particular kind of pediatric cancer.
- The justice advocate who, sometimes even at the risk of his or her life, pursues equity and fair treatment for those who have been marginalized by society.

Seen in that light, pursuit is manifestly different from dabbling or toe-dipping. It speaks of something that requires focus and energy and a level of devotion that other things in life neither get nor deserve. Yet we can also pursue lesser things—even inappropriate things. We can . . .

- Pursue a relationship that is either out of bounds or unwanted by the other party
- Pursue a career simply because it may bring a measure of fame, wealth, or notoriety
- Pursue the approval and acceptance of others—even when their approval isn't all that important

Pursuit is a thing that can be magnificent in its ideals and goals or corrupted by wrong motives or unworthy targets.

So, as followers of Christ, what is worth pursuing? And how can we make sure that what we pursue is deserving of that level of energy and emotional investment?

Perhaps a good place to start is to listen to the words of one of the most driven, passionate pursuers found in the Scriptures: Paul.

A Heart for Pursuit

When Robert F. Kennedy ran for president of the United States in 1968, he often used a line that has been attributed to George Bernard Shaw:

> Some men see things as they are and say, why? I dream things that never were and say, why not?

As a result, RFK saw things as they were—and how he believed they could be, or even *must* be. Kennedy considered the dire straits of the Black poor in the Deep South, and he was heartbroken by the sight of starving, diseased children who lived in the poorest parts of the wealthiest country on earth. This anguish was deepened by what he saw as a disproportionate number of young Black men dying in the jungles of Vietnam—in many cases because they had no other way out of poverty and despair. He was angered by the exploitation of migrant workers in the American West, and he sought to bring fairness to wage and workday expectations (or demands). He was troubled by the inhumane living conditions of Native Americans on reservations, where the young were being consumed by alcoholism and hopelessness. Kennedy built his campaign on what could be called "the least of these." His campaign became a pursuit of justice for the downtrodden, the forgotten, and the marginalized.

This pursuit not only defined RFK's campaign but also seemed to define him as well. In spite of growing up in the lap of luxury, Kennedy was able to look at someone else's hurting, deprived child and see one of his own children in that exact place—giving him empathy for those who were suffering. A pursuit fueled by empathy is a powerful thing indeed.

While far from perfect and deeply flawed, Robert Kennedy had a heart for pursuit. And he pursued progress, improvement, and change relentlessly—some would even say ruthlessly.

In a far different way, this heart of pursuit also characterized the apostle Paul. His own statements about his work in the gospel are filled with the markings of passionate pursuit.

> But I do not consider my life of any account as dear to myself, so that I may finish my course and the ministry which I received from the Lord Jesus, to testify solemnly of the gospel of God's grace. (Acts 20:24)

> And in this way I aspired to preach the gospel, not where Christ was already known by name, so that I would not build on another person's foundation. (Romans 15:20)

> For Christ did not send me to baptize, but to preach the gospel, not with cleverness of speech, so that the cross of Christ would not be made of no effect. (1 Corinthians 1:17)

> For if I preach the gospel, I have nothing to boast about, for I am under compulsion; for woe to me if I do not preach the gospel. (1 Corinthians 9:16)

"Woe to me!" What an interesting contrast to Isaiah's self-declaration of woe. Isaiah declared upon himself a woe for having lips unfit to speak of his God (Isaiah 6:5), but Paul declared a woe upon himself if he did anything *but* speak the message of the Christ! From the moment of his encounter with Jesus on the Damascus Road (see Acts 9:1–18), Saul of Tarsus saw his heart transformed. On his way to persecute and imprison followers of Christ, the young Pharisee encountered Jesus himself, and was forever changed. As the apostle Paul, he became a kind of laser-guided missile, passionate to see the gospel invade every corner of his world.

But before the Damascus Road, that heart of pursuit was misguided. Misdirected. Misapplied. And, like Kennedy, quite ruthless. Later in life, Paul confessed how flawed passionate pursuit can be when it is invested in the wrong things. He told his own story of such misguided pursuit to his friends at Philippi.

When Pursuit Is Flawed

How honest are you about your story? And by "how honest" I mean, how honest are you in how you present yourself? Do you describe yourself as:

Always asking the wise questions?
Always on top of every situation?
Always the hero of every story you tell?

One of the most colorful and controversial characters of the first half of the twentieth century was T. E. Lawrence, better known by his nom de voyage Lawrence of Arabia. A British officer assigned to Arabia during the final years of World War I, Lawrence was involved in the Arab revolt against their Ottoman rulers and in some ways helped to create the modern Arab world as we know it today. No small achievements to be sure.

However, scholars and historians who have studied Lawrence's memoir *Seven Pillars of Wisdom* claim to have uncovered dozens of embellishments and exaggerations, allegedly placed in the book by Lawrence to enhance his image. To some degree, only Lawrence fully knew where the line was between fact and fiction in his story.

So, how would you write your own story? When Paul related his story to the Philippians, it was with a candor and honesty that is almost unnerving. He spoke of a life of passionate pursuit for things that he chased with all his might, wrongly thinking they would give him right standing with his God:

> I myself could boast as having confidence even in the flesh. If anyone else thinks he is confident in the flesh, I have more reason: circumcised the eighth day, of the nation of Israel, of the tribe of Benjamin, a Hebrew of Hebrews; as to the Law, a Pharisee; as to zeal, a persecutor of the church; as to the righteousness which is in the Law, found blameless.
>
> But whatever things were gain to me, these things I have counted as loss because of Christ. (3:4–7)

These things were not all inherently evil, but they were things that of themselves could never bring Paul into relationship with God. Yes, as he says, they could make him "confident in the flesh"—but the flesh is not the solution; it is the problem. In the previous chapter we discussed the fact that the ancient world was more concerned with the community than with the individual. As such, it was important to bring honor to the community, and there were two types of such honor:

Ascribed honor: honor received and given as a result of connections to others

Achieved honor: honor given and received due to personal achievement

Where was Paul's confidence? The two things that gave him honor and allowed him to honor the community as well were the following:

His Jewish heritage. In this area, Paul is tapping into his lineage as one of God's chosen people. In verse 5, he recounts all the things that marked his life as an ethnic son of Abraham, including circumcision—the outward badge of Jewishness—as well as his national identity (Israel) and tribal membership (Benjamin), which add up to him being "a Hebrew of Hebrews." This refers to the absolute, undeniable purity of his Jewish blood. To many of us (especially in the West) such ethnic purity seems like a secondary issue at best, but such was not the case with ancient Jews.

Every time you see a genealogy in the Bible, you are not merely seeing a section of the Bible that may seem boring to read—you are seeing the absolute value Jews placed on pure blood. It's little wonder then that Matthew, the most Jewish of the Gospels, opens with the genealogy of Jesus. The genealogy answers any and all questions about Jesus's Jewish heritage, as well any concerns about His roots in the line of King David.

For Paul, all these things brought him honor—an honor ascribed to him as a son of Abraham and a Hebrew of Hebrews. He did nothing to receive it or achieve it; rather, this honor was ascribed to him through his birth and upbringing as a Jew.

His acts of pursuit. This is where we see the misdirection of the heart of Paul when he was Saul of Tarsus. He achieved honorable status and standing in the community through what he at the time saw as three accomplishments, listed in verses 5–6:

"As to the Law, a Pharisee"
"As to zeal, a persecutor of the church"
"As to the righteousness which is in the Law, found blameless"

Each of these things involved deep commitment, great energy, and passionate pursuit. Living by the law and trying to establish relationship (righteousness) through it is one thing. It is an altogether different thing, however, when he saw himself as achieving honor through the persecution of the church. He saw the imprisonment and killing of those who claimed Christ as a source of achieved honor—even bringing honor to the nation of Israel. While we see his acts against Christ followers as savage and evil, the community of Judaism saw Saul of Tarsus as a defender of the true faith. As has been said, one person's terrorist is another person's freedom fighter. A villain to the Christian community, Paul was a true champion to those of the temple and the synagogue.

Tragically, no matter how well received he was by his own people, young Saul's misguided pursuits only contributed to an ongoing hardening of his heart. Acts 9:1 describes that hardness of heart well when it says, "Meanwhile, Saul was still breathing out murderous threats against the Lord's disciples" (NIV).

It was not until he met the Lord Jesus Christ that Paul realized that everything he had been doing to achieve honor was more accurately a source of shame. Go back to the encounter Paul had with Jesus on the Damascus Road (Acts 9). When Saul of Tarsus asked the voice within the bright light to identify itself, he heard, "I am Jesus whom you are persecuting" (v. 5).

In persecuting the church, Paul was actually persecuting the very Christ who had died for him. The Son of the very God Saul of Tarsus had spent his life pursuing. Paul's words to the Philippians frame his pursuit of honor as a tragic case of misguided passion. That changed, however, after the Damascus Road. Once he met Jesus, Paul understood that the things he pursued could not provide the relationship with God he so desperately sought. His ultimate conclusion?

> But whatever things were gain to me, these things I have counted as loss because of Christ. (Philippians 3:7)

In Christ, Saul/Paul found what he had always pursued—and what a change it made in his heart, life, and values! Now the pursuit that had been flawed and often destructive would bear fruit to the honor of more than his community—this new pursuit would bring honor to God himself.

When Pursuit Is Fruitful

Tucked away in one of the major prophetical books of the Old Testament is a most valuable reminder. Jeremiah, the weeping prophet, had plenty of dark and foreboding messages to deliver to the people of God. Warnings of disaster and deportation. Warnings of judgment on rebellion.

Yet in the midst of those warnings and prophetic utterances, Jeremiah made a fascinating statement on pursuit—and what (or who) is actually worth pursuing:

> This is what the LORD says: "Let no wise man boast of his wisdom, nor let the mighty man boast of his might, nor a rich man boast of his riches; but let the one who boasts boast of this, that he understands and knows Me, that I am the LORD who exercises mercy, justice, and righteousness on the earth; for I delight in these things," declares the LORD. (9:23–24)

Jeremiah's passion was that we would pursue the infinite riches of knowing the Creator of the universe—a pursuit the late J. I. Packer described in his classic book *Knowing God.* As we have seen, many of the things we pursue are well and good. Many can be helpful and productive. Jeremiah's point was that nothing is as significant as the pursuit of God.

This is what Paul discovered on the Damascus Road. He found that the pursuit of religious achievement, ritual purity, and adherence to regulations was missing the most meaningful of all points. He could pursue all those things without ever really knowing the God his heart craved. As a result, the Jesus of Saul's persecution became the Jesus of Paul's passionate pursuit—a seismic shift in his thought processes that recalibrated his thinking, priorities, and values.

> More than that, I count all things to be loss in view of the surpassing value of knowing Christ Jesus my Lord, for

> whom I have suffered the loss of all things, and count them mere rubbish, so that I may gain Christ, and may be found in Him, not having a righteousness of my own derived from the Law, but that which is through faith in Christ, the righteousness which comes from God on the basis of faith, that I may know Him and the power of His resurrection and the fellowship of His sufferings, being conformed to His death; if somehow I may attain to the resurrection from the dead. (Philippians 3:8–11)

For Paul, an entire lifetime spent pursuing the deeds of Judaism was replaced by pursuing the relationship offered in Christ. Notice Paul's longings:

- To know Christ
- To gain Christ
- To be found in Christ
- To have righteousness from Christ

He then closes those reflections by digging deeper into that primary pursuit—knowing Christ (and through Him, the Father). His words of passion mingled with mystery are not looking for superficial acquaintance with the Christ, but rather they express a longing to experience in his life the depths of all Christ has done for him.

That is radical! *The Bible Knowledge Commentary* gives a good sense of what Paul is and is not pursuing here:

> Paul also longed to share in the fellowship of Christ's sufferings and in so doing to become like Him in His death (Philippians 3:10). These sufferings were not Christ's substitutionary sufferings on the cross. Paul knew that those could not be

> shared. But he did desire to participate with Christ, since he was one of His, in suffering for the sake of righteousness (cf. 1:29). God had used Ananias to tell Paul that this is precisely what he would do as a servant of Christ (Acts 9:16). The apostle did indeed suffer for Christ because he represented Him so openly and truly (cf. Rom. 8:36; 2 Cor. 4:10).

I have to admit that Paul's pursuit of Christ—even to the point of sharing in His suffering—is daunting. It forces me to examine my own pursuit of the Savior and the degree to which I really want to enter into His sufferings. But again, Paul is the very definition of passionate, and he becomes an extraordinary reminder of what it really looks like when someone wants to know the Lord with his or her whole being.

Dwight Lyman Moody (1837–99), the well-known evangelist of the late 1800s, made famous the saying, "The world has yet to see what God will do with a man fully consecrated to Him." I wonder. It seems to me that, at least to some degree, when we see the all-in, nonstop, absolute commitment of the apostle Paul—a person God used to turn the world upside down (Acts 17:6)—we may just see how powerfully God can work when a life is well and truly given over to Him for His purposes.

This pursuit is profoundly fruitful, because it transforms people fundamentally—impacting not just how they think and feel but also how they live out the heart of Christ. This is the fruit of knowing Him, and it wonderfully puts Jeremiah's challenge into a New Testament context that we can aspire to as well. Notice this observation by the late Warren Wiersbe in his *Bible Exposition Commentary*:

> When he became a Christian, it was not the end for Paul, but the beginning. His experience with Christ was so tremendous that it transformed his life. And this experience continued in the years to follow. It was a personal experience ("That I may know Him") as Paul walked with Christ, prayed, obeyed His will, and sought to glorify His name. When he was living under Law, all Paul had was a set of rules. But now he had a Friend, a Master, a constant Companion!

No wonder the apostle said that everything he had gained according to the flesh was without value when compared to knowing Christ (see Philippians 3:4–8). This was a passion worth pursuing!

When Pursuit Is Focused

Many US sports fans will remember when professional basketball player Michael Jordan decided to try his hand at baseball—one of MJ's lifelong loves. Although one of the greatest players of all time in his chosen sport and one of the greatest athletes of his generation, Jordan struggled to progress in his baseball career.

It just didn't make any sense—until I heard an analysis by a baseball writer. He said that what made Jordan great on the basketball court hindered his effectiveness on the ball diamond—his remarkable peripheral vision. The ability to scan the court to find the open man and deliver a killer assist was a big part of Jordan's game, but that same peripheral vision impeded his ability to focus totally on a pitched baseball—which is absolutely vital if you are to pick up the spin and rotation of the ball so you can identify the pitch and understand how to most successfully attack it.

Eventually, Jordan abandoned the experiment and returned to the NBA, where he was once again great—maybe even the GOAT (greatest of all time). In the end, his baseball career may have been hindered by a problem with focus.

The apostle Paul had no such struggle. His focus was so absolute that in considering the walk with Christ that had supplanted his former commitment to Judaism, he wrote this to the Christians at Philippi:

> Not that I have already grasped it all or have already become perfect, but I press on if I may also take hold of that for which I was even taken hold of by Christ Jesus. Brothers and sisters, I do not regard myself as having taken hold of it yet; but **one thing** I do: forgetting what lies behind and reaching forward to what lies ahead, I press on toward the goal for the prize of the upward call of God in Christ Jesus. (3:12–14)

One thing. A pursued thing. A focused thing. While acknowledging that he has not yet arrived, Paul affirms that he is still in pursuit. And the one thing he pursues is the continuation of his pursuit of Jesus: "I press on toward the goal for the prize of the upward call of God in Christ Jesus" (v. 14).

This pursuit—Paul's one thing—involves setting aside the things of the past (already described in vv. 4–7) and reaching forward to what lies ahead. But in the end, it is about pursuing Christ and the prize that awaits.

Throughout the Scriptures we see extraordinary things happen when people pursue the things of God ahead of their own priorities:

Noah built an ark against the coming floods.
Abram left his home to follow God's call to a land he did not know.
Moses left the relative safety of the Midian desert and returned to Egypt to face Pharaoh.
Hannah risked the mockery and misunderstanding of Eli, the priest, in her prayer-filled desire for a child—a child who would become God's prophet for Israel.
Elijah faced the prophets of Baal in a Mount Carmel showdown.
Daniel faced up to kings and conquerors, refusing to compromise his convictions.

The examples could go on and on, but they are not limited to Bible characters. Wiersbe shares a helpful anecdote:

> Too many Christians are too involved in "many things," when the secret of progress is to concentrate on "one thing." It was this decision that was a turning point in Dwight L. Moody's life. Before the tragedy of the Chicago fire in 1871, Mr. Moody was involved in Sunday school promotion, YMCA work, evangelistic meetings, and many other activities; but after the fire, he determined to devote himself exclusively to evangelism. "This one thing I do!" became a reality to him. As a result, millions of people heard the gospel.

It doesn't mean that the many things are sinful or evil or even wrong. It means that much of our effectiveness for Christ and growth in Him comes from a willingness to focus on the things that matter most—the things that call us forward in Him. It is the focus and pursuit captured by the words of the letter to the Hebrews:

> Therefore, since we also have such a great cloud of witnesses surrounding us, let's rid ourselves of every obstacle and the sin which so easily entangles us, and let's run with endurance the race that is set before us, looking only at Jesus, the originator and perfecter of the faith, who for the joy set before Him endured the cross, despising the shame, and has sat down at the right hand of the throne of God. (12:1–2)

"Looking only at Jesus." Now, that is a focused pursuit! Helen Lemmel's classic devotional hymn expresses both the pursuit and the focus Paul's heart desired:

> O soul, are you weary and troubled?
> No light in the darkness you see?
> There's light for a look at the Savior,
> And life more abundant and free!
>
> Through death into life everlasting,
> He passed, and we follow Him there;
> O'er us sin no more hath dominion—
> For more than conqu'rors we are!
>
> Turn your eyes upon Jesus,
> Look full in His wonderful face,
> And the things of earth will grow strangely dim,
> In the light of His glory and grace.

Questions for Personal Reflection or Group Discussion

1. What are some things you have pursued in your life? Were they good or bad (or perhaps even neutral)? To what degree did they give you the fulfillment you sought?

2. As you consider your life to this point, what are some things that are sources of ascribed honor? What are some things that have brought you achieved honor? In whose eyes was that honor achieved?
3. If you were writing your own story, how would you describe yourself? How comfortable are you with being honest about your shortcomings? Are there times when it isn't appropriate to be utterly candid about such things?
4. Paul saw himself as a defender of Judaism, yet he used that value as justification to do great harm to others. Have you ever felt justified in mistreating others? Was that justification legitimate, even if your actions weren't?
5. What are some ways you could develop a more focused pursuit of Jesus? What might that look like?

4

FOCUSING ON A NECESSARY THING

> But the Lord answered and said to her, "Martha, Martha, you are worried and distracted by many things; but only ***one thing*** is necessary."
>
> Luke 10:41–42

At the beginning of the COVID-19 pandemic crisis in 2020, one of the most commonly heard terms was *essential.* A reshuffling of the societal deck took place, redefining what was essential and what was, at least for the short term, optional (if not downright unnecessary). How people defined what was and what wasn't essential was a major sticking point, but some things became clear. In addition to the hardworking medical personnel, the importance of farmers, truckers, service workers, and people in a plethora of other lines of work that, perhaps, had been undervalued before was suddenly remembered. And the celebrities, entertainers, and athletes who had dominated the news media were suddenly recognized to be less vital.

The realities of the coronavirus also forced a recalibration on a personal level that matched the upheaval within society—and that was true of us as well. Marlene and I have always sought to find the necessary wisdom to discern needs from wants, but when restaurants closed and stores had empty shelves (especially in the toilet paper area), it was easy to see where people were placing value. Whereas before the pandemic, church attendance seemed to some like a duty at best and an annoyance at worst, many followers of Christ began to crave the corporate fellowship and worship that perhaps they had taken for granted before the crisis began. While I'm absolutely thankful for the amazing technology of our day, sitting in your pajamas and watching a livestream of a church service presented in an empty auditorium just isn't the same as a group of Christ followers joining together to sing "Amazing Grace" or "10,000 Reasons (Bless the Lord)."

In that season of crisis, some things were necessary and essential. Other things simply weren't—regardless of how much those things dominated our thinking prior to the pandemic.

I think the kind of critical thinking forced upon us by COVID-19 is actually a very healthy thing. Imagine that—healthy thinking coming out of a health crisis. Amazing. As life slowly began to return to something like normal, this was one of the major questions: Will our definitions of need versus want and essential versus unnecessary revert to where we were before, or have we learned something very important through that experience? Is all this learning sticky enough to impact our lives going forward, or will it be relegated to the past as soon as possible?

One of my favorite expressions is "the things that matter most." When you read that phrase, what kinds of things come to your mind?

Family? Purpose? Spiritual growth? Other things?

What are some of the things that don't matter most but that we can treat as if they do matter most?

Hobbies? Success? Money? Entertainment? Other things?

We all have our own lists in answer to those questions. However, from the perspective of the follower of Christ, taking this kind of spiritual inventory is a healthy thing to do—even if a global pandemic pushes us into it.

But while we consider what is essential and necessary versus things that are of perhaps lesser significance, allow me to raise one further question: Is it possible that we can incorrectly make spiritual service one of the things that matters most? What if we're wrong and there is something else that is more essential? More necessary?

That brings into focus the one thing we want to consider in this chapter. While not devaluing the privilege and responsibility of spiritual service, Jesus certainly places this next one thing within a perspective of something that matters even more. We see that in Luke 10:38–42:

> Now as they were traveling along, He entered a village; and a woman named Martha welcomed Him into her home. And she had a sister called Mary, who was also seated at the Lord's feet, and was listening to His word. But Martha was distracted with all her preparations; and she came up to Him and said, "Lord, do You not care that my sister has left

> me to do the serving by myself? Then tell her to help me." But the Lord answered and said to her, "Martha, Martha, you are worried and distracted by many things; but only **one thing** is necessary; for Mary has chosen the good part, which shall not be taken away from her."

"One thing is necessary." Not optional. Not superfluous. Necessary. That certainly sounds like something worth exploring together.

An Important Value

I've commented before in previous writings that for many years Marlene has encouraged me to partake heavily of home-improvement shows on TV. You know the kind, where a couple looks at a house and presents their list of "must-haves" (talk about essential versus nonessential). The list usually includes things like an open-concept floor plan, granite countertops, a gas fireplace, stainless-steel appliances, and more. And more. And more.

What usually knocks me off-balance, though, is that one of the "must-haves" these prospective buyers consistently clamor for is a large space for entertaining. Maybe I'm just a curmudgeon or a hermit. Maybe I'm just not much of a people person. Maybe I'm a throwback to the days of the mountain men who would crawl up into the woods and the wilderness and not see another human being for two years.

But I listen to these people talk about all the entertaining they want to do, and I wonder, Who are all these people who are being entertained? Where do people find the time to do all this entertaining? And perhaps my biggest question: Who buys a house based on whether or not you can entertain in it?

Not me.

Seriously, I know many people really enjoy entertaining, and that's fine. There certainly isn't anything wrong with it. In fact, hospitality (a more old-school term for entertaining) was a tremendously high value in the ancient Middle East, and it continues to be important there today. Specifically for our purposes, in ancient Jewish culture hospitality was very significant, and it was one of two primary ways a woman could gain honor and status in a community.

In our culture, it is almost unthinkable how undervalued women were in the ancient world—but it is true. They had virtually no rights and no opportunities. So how could a woman achieve a status of honor within her community? Either a woman gave her husband children (preferably sons) or she became valued for her ability to care for the visitors and dignitaries that arrived in the community—in other words, hospitality.

This brings us right into the home of Martha of Bethany. In Luke 10, immediately following Jesus's telling of the parable of the good Samaritan, the Master and His followers arrive at Martha's home. There, Martha would sacrificially care for her guests as the Samaritan cared for the man left for dead on the side of the road. Now, as a matter of full disclosure, I'm a Martha fan (I have a whole chapter on her in my book *The Spotlight of Faith*). I personally think she is one of the most consistently misrepresented characters in the Scriptures. I have been on a crusade (and I'm not alone in this quest) to bring some equity to how Martha is presented, because Luke 10 is routinely seen as the Martha story—usually to the absolute neglect of John 11, where we clearly see the spiritual progress Martha has made.

But that's not the point here. In Luke 10, we see Martha as an apparently single woman; verse 38 says she welcomes Jesus into *her* home—which may mean that she was widowed and her husband left the house to her. As she welcomes Jesus and the Twelve into her home, it is with the understanding that He is one of the most, if not *the* most, celebrated personalities of the day. Jesus's arrival in the village of Bethany was a huge honor to the community. And Jesus's coming to the home of Martha was a huge responsibility that she bore in the eyes of that community.

For Jesus to visit their small village was stunning. For Martha to represent the entire community by showing hospitality to the miracle-working Rabbi meant that she was under intense pressure. We discussed earlier (in chapter 2) that those of us in the modern West live in cultures dominated by individualism. We rise and fall based on what we do, and often we are trained to say, "I don't care what anyone else thinks."

Ancient Israel was a drastically different kind of culture. It mattered greatly what other people thought. How people conducted themselves reflected on their family and their entire community. If you brought dishonor to your community, you could quickly find yourself on the outside looking in without any way back into the village's good graces. You became an outsider. A pariah. An outcast.

As Martha welcomed Jesus into her home, there was much more at stake than simply providing some snacks for weary travelers. Going forward, her standing in the community would be driven by whether or not she brought honor to her community in the hospitality she showed to the celebrity Teacher who had come to town.

So, in Luke's account, we see two things—one that is normal and one that is very unusual. Notice again 10:38–40:

> Now as they were traveling along, He entered a village; and a woman named Martha welcomed Him into her home. And she had a sister called Mary, who was also seated at the Lord's feet, and was listening to His word. But Martha was distracted with all her preparations.

What is normal and expected is that Martha is busy—distracted even—with her preparations. This is not surprising given what we have seen about the high value placed on hospitality and the sense of community investment in the entire event. We would certainly expect her to be busy preparing for her guests.

What is unusual and unexpected is for her sister, Mary, to be sitting at Jesus's feet listening to Him teach. This is the posture of a disciple. In the book of Acts, the apostle Paul defends his rabbinic pedigree by asserting,

> I am indeed a Jew, born in Tarsus of Cilicia, but brought up in this city at the feet of Gamaliel, taught according to the strictness of our fathers' law, and was zealous toward God as you all are today. (22:3 NKJV)

"At the feet of Gamaliel" is a statement of how he was taught and trained in the Scriptures. Here we see Mary seated at Jesus's feet! In a time when women did not naturally receive significant opportunities for spiritual learning and growth, Mary is welcomed by Jesus to take the place of a disciple and sit at His feet to learn from His teaching—a situation that would have been shocking to the community. Women were not included in such spiritual endeavors as discipling. Mary was a woman taking a man's place in a culture where that was absolutely not allowed—except with Jesus. In fact, a number of women were part of the group that accompanied the Savior on His travels:

> Soon afterward, Jesus began going around from one city and village to another, proclaiming and preaching the kingdom of God. The twelve were with Him, and also some women who had been healed of evil spirits and sicknesses: Mary who was called Magdalene, from whom seven demons had gone out, and Joanna the wife of Chuza, Herod's steward, and Susanna, and many others who were contributing to their support out of their private means. (Luke 8:1–3)

Now, Luke adds two more women to Jesus's story, and the contrast between these two sisters from Bethany is dramatic. Martha is playing the role that the culture not only expects of her but also will evaluate and measure her by. Mary is almost in an "I don't care what people think" scenario. She takes a man's place and sits as a disciple before Jesus so she can learn and grow. At this point, it is Martha who raises the point of conflict. And remember, she is doing exactly what she is expected to do.

A Legitimate Complaint

The house was a shambles. In fact, it was hard to tell how it was even standing, let alone being lived in. In addition to the house being rundown and virtually derelict, the yard and gardens were overrun and looked more like a jungle than a residence in a suburban neighborhood. For years, the house had continued to deteriorate, and its decline was obvious—even to the point of impacting the property values of the surrounding homeowners. Finally, after months of hoping for the situation to improve, the neighbors joined together to file a complaint with the city.

It was an absolutely legitimate complaint.

But was it an appropriate one?

What the neighbors had failed to learn was that the homeowner of the derelict house was barely surviving on a fixed income while battling several debilitating illnesses that made it impossible for him to do anything involving physical activity. Their complaint resulted in their ill and financially challenged neighbor being shamed, which did nothing to actually solve the problem.

Not all legitimate complaints are appropriate complaints. And that is where we find Martha.

> But Martha was distracted with all her preparations; and she came up to Him and said, "Lord, do You not care that my sister has left me to do the serving by myself? Then tell her to help me." (Luke 10:40)

It is hard to know with certainty what the full measure of Martha's complaint actually was. It is likely, however, that her complaint was a two-edged sword. First, and most obviously, Martha was involved in the culturally important work of hospitality, and with so much at stake, it is not surprising that Martha needed help in preparing for the large group that had crowded into her home. And it is not at all surprising that she expected that help to come from her sister, Mary. Martha even goes so far as to instruct Jesus to instruct Mary to do that very thing!

The second aspect of the complaint, however, is a bit more subtle. It may be that, as much as Martha resented being left to do all the work, she also resented the fact that Mary was assuming a man's place—creating a scandal within the community whose favor she was seeking to earn. Martha, while working to provide a level of hospitality that would give her greater honor in the village, may have feared that this very honor was threatened by her sister's culturally unacceptable behavior.

Such concerns were deemed absolutely appropriate in that day and time and place. But Martha's underlying emotion actually takes a seemingly legitimate complaint and makes it inappropriate. Notice again how she prefaces that complaint: "Lord, do You not care?" (v. 40).

It is one thing for Martha to question the actions of her sister, but it's another thing altogether for her to question the heart of Jesus. In fact, the question that underlies her complaint may have resonated with Jesus's male disciples who filled her house. Do you recall the story in Mark 4 when Jesus and His men were crossing the Sea of Galilee in a small fishing boat? A vicious storm began to whip across that body of water. Exhausted from a draining day of ministry, Jesus was asleep in the boat. Terrified at the intensity of the storm, the disciples awakened their sleeping Teacher and asked Him a question that sounds Martha-esque: "Teacher, do You not care that we are perishing?" (v. 38).

"Do You not care?" That is one question we can never legitimately level at the Son of God. The very fact that Jesus was in Martha's dusty village and working His way toward a cross in Jerusalem was enduring evidence of a care that was more than just concern for a boat ride in a storm or the preparation of a communal meal. His care in all the little things rose from the wellspring of a love and compassion that was incapable of not caring.

Martha's complaint was legitimate in the issue it addressed, but it was tragically off base when considering the heart and spirit that birthed that complaint.

A Necessary Correction

Just as COVID-19 created an opportunity to correct some (many?) of our misapplied concerns, values, and priorities, the incident at Martha's house also created an opportunity for correction:

> But the Lord answered and said to her, "Martha, Martha, you are worried and distracted by many things; but only **one thing** is necessary; for Mary has chosen the good part, which shall not be taken away from her." (Luke 10:41–42)

In this moment of correction we find the one thing Martha needed to come to grips with. The necessary thing. The truly essential thing. We must first understand that Jesus is not saying Martha's concerns are unimportant. The Master is not unaware of the culture and its expectations. He is not inconsiderate of the effort and labor involved in preparing a meal. And He is not unappreciative of her service and her desire to provide for Him and His followers. At no point does the Master hint that her service is unimportant.

However, while not unimportant, Martha's concerns do not represent in this moment what is most important. "One thing is necessary." What Mary was doing had higher value than what Martha was concerned for. What, then, was the one necessary thing, and why did it matter so much?

In reality, there are differences of opinion as to what made Mary's actions the necessary ones. Some have speculated that perhaps Mary was simply doing what Jesus had invited people to do in His great invitation. We know that His Great Commandment was for us to love God and love our neighbors (Matthew 22:36–40) and His Great Commission was to take the gospel to the whole world (28:19–20). But what was His great invitation?

> Come to Me, all who are weary and burdened, and I will give you rest. Take My yoke upon you and learn from Me, for I am gentle and humble in heart, and you will find rest for your souls. For My yoke is comfortable, and My burden is light. (11:28–30)

Jesus's great invitation was to come to Him and learn from Him—exactly what Mary was doing at that moment! Perhaps, some argue, Mary's choice was superior because she was doing what has immeasurable value—learning of the Master at His own feet.

That may be so, but others argue for a more timeless principle. None of us can sit at Jesus's literal feet as Mary did, but we can all cultivate hearts of devotion for Him by placing the highest spiritual value on knowing Him more and more. We saw in chapter 3 that Paul wrote of this, saying that he longed to "know Him and the power of His resurrection and the fellowship of His sufferings"

(Philippians 3:10). Paul, the apostle to the gentiles who had learned at the feet of Gamaliel, would have been extremely comfortable learning at Jesus's feet as well.

As such, some speculate that Mary was making spiritual growth a matter of higher concern than temporal service. I can relate to that. I have spent my entire adult life in vocational Christian ministry, yet I must confess that many times it's much easier to do things for God than it is to sit in His presence and allow my heart to be shaped by His infinite being. In many ways, it's much easier to be active with Bible study and meetings and counseling appointments and church administration than it is to hear Him beckon our hearts with the call to "stop striving and know that I am God" (Psalm 46:10).

Now, don't misunderstand. Spiritual service is important. In fact, Ephesians 2:10 tells us, "For we are His workmanship, created in Christ Jesus for good works, which God prepared beforehand so that we would walk in them."

In our new birth, we've been created for the very purpose of accomplishing good things, and those things, like Martha's service, matter very much. However, the truest and most meaningful spiritual service doesn't evidence itself in endless activity for activity's sake. The best and truest spiritual service flows from our relationship with Him. Our walk with God creates both the motivation and the empowering for the good works that we have been created to accomplish in Christ—but those works in and of themselves can never create a deepening, growing relationship with God.

This is not the proverbial "Which came first, the chicken or the egg?" situation. Relationship precedes service. Always. This may be the exact reason for Jesus's words to Martha.

"One thing is necessary"—that we cultivate, strengthen, deepen, and enrich our relationship with our Lord. That alone gives meaning and purpose to our acts of service. That deepening relationship is absolutely what matters most.

Far from being a rebuke, however, Jesus's words to Martha are a personal expression of that great invitation to come into His presence and learn of Him and from Him. And there is no better place to be than right there!

The apostle James wrote, "Come close to God and He will come close to you" (4:8). Mary did—and Jesus was inviting Martha to join her in this one necessary thing. How would she respond? In my opinion, her response is evidenced in her confident trust in Jesus even after He didn't respond to her cry for help when her brother, Lazarus, was dying. When Jesus arrives once again in Bethany, days after Lazarus died, she affirms her assurance of His identity—*before* Lazarus is restored to life (see John 11).

I would suggest to you that in the time between Luke 10 and John 11, Martha had learned to sit at the feet of Jesus with Mary. She had learned to cease striving. She had learned to know that He is God—and her learning is evidenced in her confession in John 11:27: "Yes, Lord; I have come to believe that You are the Christ, the Son of God, and He who comes into the world." She had taken hold of the one necessary thing.

Some say the lyrics were birthed in the slave fields of the antebellum South, and others say they were created in the jazz corners of New Orleans. No one really knows for sure who penned the words, but the first verse of "Just a Closer Walk with Thee" captures the heart of Mary's contentment at Jesus's feet, and the second verse underscores the Savior's words of loving correction to the busy, distracted Martha.

> I am weak, but Thou art strong;
> Jesus, keep me from all wrong;
> I'll be satisfied as long
> As I walk, let me walk close to Thee.
>
> Through this world of toil and snares,
> If I falter, Lord, who cares?
> Who with me my burden shares?
> None but Thee, dear Lord, none but Thee.
>
> Just a closer walk with Thee,
> Grant it, Jesus, is my plea,
> Daily walking close to Thee,
> Let it be, dear Lord, let it be.

The one necessary thing . . . a life lived in the presence and provision of the living Christ. Yes, let it be, dear Lord, let it be.

Questions for Personal Reflection or Group Discussion

1. What are some things you view as essential? Unnecessary? How have seasons of trial or hardship challenged those values? How have such times impacted your view of people and their relative importance in today's world?

2. What are things you look to to give you honor or value in your own eyes? In the eyes of others? What is the danger of finding value in those things? What could be the benefits of seeking a life worthy of honor?
3. Paul learned at the feet of Gamaliel, and Mary learned at the feet of Jesus. Who has been a mentor to you, so you could say that, metaphorically, you have learned at their feet? Has anyone been able to learn at your feet?
4. Which do you find easier—building your relationship with the Lord or doing acts of service in His name? Why? In what way does this tendency help you pursue or ignore the one necessary thing of knowing Him more deeply and personally?
5. How do you normally respond to being challenged? To being rebuked? Do you bristle and become defensive, or do you take it to heart as an opportunity to learn? How can you improve your normal response?

5

FOCUSING ON A DESIRED THING

One thing I have asked from the LORD, that I shall seek.

Psalm 27:4

Field of Dreams is one of my favorite baseball movies, although in reality it isn't about baseball. Baseball is merely the vehicle for telling a story about the relationships between fathers and sons. But I digress. In *Field of Dreams* there's a classic scene where the main character, Ray Kinsella, goes to Boston to take former author and social activist Terence Mann to Fenway Park for a Boston Red Sox game. They enter the main concourse of the stadium in mid conversation about Mann's general disillusionment with the state of the culture when Kinsella stops and asks, "So, what do you want?"

Mann launches into a lengthy soliloquy about the pain

he has endured and the ignominy he has faced, and he finally says that basically he just wants to be left alone. Kinsella, with a wry smile, points to the concession stand before them and says, "No, I meant, what do you want?"

In both the big things and the small things of life, we are often driven by what we want. By desire.

The desire for a relationship.

The desire for a career.

The desire for recognition.

The desire for wealth.

The desire for security.

The desire for social change.

The desire for improved health.

Desire is the ultimate answer to the question, What do you want? And what we desire is often one of the most revealing things about us. While many of the desires that fill our hearts are good and worthwhile, sometimes our deepest desires reveal something in us that is extremely dark.

The desire to dominate others.

The desire for satisfaction at the expense of others.

The desire for illicit pleasure by using others.

The desire for the hurt of others.

So, desire can sometimes unveil us in uncomfortable ways. But when our desires are raised to the highest place, we long for what is the best of all true longings. French physicist, mathematician, and theologian Blaise Pascal famously captured the truest and deepest desire of the human heart in his *Pensées*, where he wrote:

> What else does this craving, and this helplessness, proclaim but that there was once in man a true happiness, of which

> all that now remains is the empty print and trace? This he tries in vain to fill with everything around him, seeking in things that are not there the help he cannot find in those that are, though none can help, since this infinite abyss can be filled only with an infinite and immutable object; in other words by God himself.

In *Confessions*, St. Augustine expressed it this way: "You have made us for yourself, O Lord, and our hearts are restless until they rest in you."

C. S. Lewis, one of the truly significant apologists and thinkers of the twentieth century, explored the darker side of the drive of desire in *Mere Christianity*, when he said:

> All that we call human history—money, poverty, ambition, war, prostitution, classes, empires, slavery—[is] the long terrible story of man trying to find something other than God which will make him happy.

Indeed, desire is clearly a powerful force. How can desire be best utilized, and even more importantly, how can it be best satisfied? Psalm 27 offers us an answer as the psalmist David presents the one thing he desires above all else.

Setting the Stage

Whenever we consider one of the psalms, it's helpful to see if the short note at the beginning of the psalm (what scholars call the psalm's superscription) can set the context of the events that prompted the writing of that song or prayer. In this case, we are left a bit wanting. While we are told that David is the author of Psalm 27, we are not given any background for it. The lyrics themselves, however, may offer us a clue.

The dominant themes of Psalm 27 are opposition from enemies (v. 2) and hope in God's rescue (v. 1). This has caused scholars to speculate that Psalm 27 may have been written while David was being pursued by Saul in his younger years, or while he was being hunted and hounded by his son Absalom in his later years. King Saul saw David as a usurper to his throne, while Absalom seemed to have lost confidence in his father's ability to rule. Does Psalm 27 land in these turbulent seasons of David's life? This certainly is possible, as it is with many of David's psalms. When pursued by Saul, he wrote Psalms 34, 52, 59, and 63, and when pursued by Absalom he wrote Psalm 3—and those are just the psalms he specifically identified as being prompted by those times when he was hunted. It may be that Psalm 27 fits that category as well.

What matters most, however, is that in the midst of the threats he faced, David trusted in God for his rescue. In fact, the contrast of danger and hope is so vivid that some scholars see Psalm 27 as two different psalms—a psalm of confident hope (vv. 1–6) and a song of lament (vv. 7–14). Such a division, however, isn't necessary. Many of David's psalms present a mixture of worship and lament, and Psalm 27 is in harmony with that pattern.

What truly sets Psalm 27 apart is that when David was being pursued by his enemies, his response was to run to the place of worship. At the time of David's writing, the temple had not been built, but the place of worship (the tabernacle) was still regarded as a symbol of the presence of God among His people. This concept caused the psalmist to flee to the place of worship as a sanctuary of safety and protection from his enemies, and to come face-to-face with his God in that place of worship.

This is where we find David's one thing. In the place of worship at a time when his life is under threat, David enters. And his hopeful faith is energized by the power and presence of the God of heaven.

Seeing the Light

One night when his life was in shambles, country music star Hank Williams Sr. was being driven home from a concert by his mother. Lying drunk in the back seat of the car, he heard his mother say, "I just saw the light"—announcing that they were close to their destination. That phrase captured his attention, and he wrote what would become the iconic country song "I Saw the Light." Williams's biographer, Colin Escott, wrote of the song, "It was the prayer of the backslider, who lives in hope of redemption."

In his own season of dark struggles, David also sought rescue and discovered much-needed light in the place of worship:

> The Lord is my light and my salvation;
> Whom should I fear?
> The Lord is the defense of my life;
> Whom should I dread?
> When evildoers came upon me to devour my flesh,
> My adversaries and my enemies, they stumbled and fell.
> If an army encamps against me,

My heart will not fear;
If war arise against me,
in spite of this I am confident. (Psalm 27:1–3)

Light is symbolic of all that is pure and good. It represents what is true in contrast to what is false. So powerful is the truth and beauty of light that the Prince of Darkness seeks to commandeer it. Paul wrote, "No wonder, for even Satan disguises himself as an angel of light" (2 Corinthians 11:14). Light is powerful, and while our spiritual enemy may attempt to counterfeit it, nothing and no one can ultimately reproduce the power of the light of the Lord.

David finds reason for confidence in this because it is more than the light of the Lord that is in view—the Lord himself is his light. David's confidence is not in himself, his strength, or even his faith, but in the God he trusts. He describes his God with strong and robust word pictures: light, salvation (deliverance or rescue), defense. He sees God as the only One he can trust to chase away the darkness that engulfs him, rescue him from the danger that surrounds him, and protect him from the enemies that pursue him. Yet, it is the imagery of light that grabs our attention—because we all have had our times of wrestling with the darkness.

As such, many of us are well familiar with the phrase "the dark night of the soul"—a word picture first penned in a poem by the Spanish mystic St. John of the Cross (1542–91). The phrase captures a sense of hopelessness understood by anyone who knows how devastating the most difficult of life experiences can be. On the Ligonier Ministries website, the late theologian R. C. Sproul wrote of the dark night of the soul:

> This phenomenon describes a malady that the greatest of Christians have suffered from time to time. It was the malady that provoked David to soak his pillow with tears. It was the malady that earned for Jeremiah the sobriquet, "The Weeping Prophet." It was the malady that so afflicted Martin Luther that his melancholy threatened to destroy him. This is no ordinary fit of depression, but it is a depression that is linked to a crisis of faith, a crisis that comes when one senses the absence of God or gives rise to a feeling of abandonment by Him.

In the dark night of the soul, we crave light—light that brings reason for hope. And that is not just true of David's fear of those who hated him with a murderous hate; we can also experience the same despair and feel the same crisis of faith. Darkness, whether actual darkness or metaphorical darkness, can put us in a very bad place.

However, whatever may be the source of the darkness that surrounds us, there is no substitute for the light that brings hope. And while there may be many sources of the darkness we experience, there is one enduring, eternal source we can flee to for the light we crave. We see that in particular in the New Testament where one of the overarching themes of John's writings is light (see John 1:7–9; 12:35–36, 46; 1 John 1:5). In John's gospel, Jesus penetrates the dark life situations of a man born blind (see chapter 2 of this book) and a woman caught in the act of adultery. In both of those encounters, Jesus identifies himself as "the Light of the world" (8:12, 9:5). His light brought forgiveness and restoration to the woman and literal light to the darkened eyes of a man who had never known sight. We too celebrate the light that we have found in Jesus, the

Light of the World, just as David celebrated the light he had sought in the place of worship.

The second half of Psalm 27 (vv. 7–14) describes the depth of the darkness—but the first half of the song front-loads that experience with the light that brings a liberating confidence to the moment of grave danger. In the presence of the Lord of light, David speaks boldly of his trust in God with phrases that stand in stark contrast to the very real dangers that have rallied against him:

> Whom should I fear?
> Whom should I dread?
> My heart will not fear.
> I am confident. (see vv. 1–3)

This is the profound sense of confidence that comes when matchless light invades our experience of darkness. And David finds it in the sanctuary—in the presence of his God. His is a God who is worthy of trust, and David's resulting confident cry resonates with the words of the apostle Paul: "What then shall we say to these things? If God is for us, who is against us?" (Romans 8:31).

Living in the Light

One of the great commercial battlegrounds of the fast-paced era of inventors and inventions that marked the late nineteenth century and early twentieth century was the race to design the coming electrical grid. Thomas Edison of New Jersey and George Westinghouse from New York (with technical assistance from Nikola Tesla) had two very different ideas about how electricity should operate in the United States. While Westinghouse and Tesla favored the alternating current model, Edison built his strategy around a direct current system.

The conflict became extremely bitter (and expensive), yet at the heart of their conflict was a common desire—to provide electricity to the homes, neighborhoods, and communities that would instantly be transformed (which would also produce huge profits). With electrical light came a newfound warmth in homes, a greater sense of safety, and an ability to function more effectively for longer hours. Living in light made a huge difference in the day-to-day experiences of the people then, while setting the stage for a twentieth century filled with creativity, entrepreneurship, and technological advances.

The power of light transforms both lives and lifestyles. And having declared the Lord himself as his light, David expresses his one thing—the thing he desires above all else is not only to *know* that light but also to *live* in it.

It's important to remember that David was a deeply flawed man. His many psalms are most often characterized by lament—crying out of deep despair for all that was wrong not only in the world but especially in his own personal world. His sins against Bathsheba (and perhaps other women as well) are sometimes viewed as the exception in David's life, but the reality of the biblical narrative says differently. David experienced great trouble and lived through immense struggles, often problems of his own making. In other words, he was very much like us.

But also like us, David had his moments. Seasons of great faith. Times of both wonderful inspiration and driving aspiration. Psalm 27:4 is, in my judgment at least, one of David's finest moments. Notice how his singular passion blossoms into a devotion for the Lord that is almost alarming in our day of casual faith and carefree discipleship:

> **One thing** I have asked from the LORD, that I
> shall seek:
> That I may dwell in the house of the LORD all
> the days of my life,
> To behold the beauty of the LORD
> And to meditate in His temple.

This is what David seeks! This one thing: to know and experience God's presence, goodness, and provision throughout his life—especially in times of turbulence and threat. The one thing David desires is what defines him as a man after God's heart (1 Samuel 13:14)—in spite of his unfortunate record of failings, shortcomings, and sin. Here, David declares that his greatest desire is not only to experience the presence, protection, and favor of the Lord but also to dwell in it!

His passion for living in the light of the Lord explodes into a full-orbed desire—David's one thing. It is so intense that it can only be expressed in a triad of devotional longings. Any of these three passions would be a worthy life goal in its own right. Yet David's one thing is so all-consuming that here, in one of his best moments, he combines them together to express his heart.

Dwell in the house of the Lord: Again, in David's day, the tabernacle was considered the house of the Lord—the tent that had been built at the base of Mount Sinai during the time of Israel's exodus from Egypt to the promised land. This literal tent—center of worship that it was—symbolized God's presence among His people. David wanted to dwell there, no doubt like the prophetess Anna who, hundreds of years later, seems to have literally lived in the temple grounds in Jerusalem (Luke 2:36–38).

Dwelling in the house of the Lord was such an important idea to David that in Psalm 27:4 he states his desire to stay there "all the days of [his] life." In his most famous psalm he declares an even more expansive desire—"dwelling . . . in the house of the LORD *forever*" (23:6; emphasis added).

What might this look like for those who follow Jesus? It begins with the declaration of John in the prologue to his gospel when he describes Jesus as the Word (1:1). However, this Word that was with God and was God is also the Word who "became flesh, and dwelt among us" (v. 14). What makes that so significant? The word translated as "dwelt" literally means "tabernacled." Just as the tabernacle represented the Father's presence to Israel (Exodus 40:34), Jesus himself came in a tent of humanity to live among His fallen creation.

The result of Jesus's tabernacling in human flesh is perhaps best seen as a two-directional blessing. On the part of our Lord, when we place our faith in Jesus, He comes to dwell in us (literally, "to take up residence in us"; see Ephesians 3:17), and the Holy Spirit likewise dwells in us (John 14:16–17). Although it is a biblical truth we hear repeatedly, it is nonetheless breathtaking that the Lord of the universe chooses to dwell in us!

The second part, however, is more closely aligned with David's one thing. We are called to abide in Christ in the same way that a branch abides in its vine (15:1–11). That constant connection provides life, sustenance, and strength, and as we abide in Christ we find in Him all that David was longing for in his desire to "dwell in the house of the Lord." Amazing as it may be, our life in the presence of Christ is rooted in a full and eternal relationship; it is not limited to a particular location or season of life.

Behold the beauty of the Lord: What is "the beauty of the Lord"? It is generally seen as the way that God expresses His favor and goodness upon His people (Exodus 34:5–6). But Bible scholar Matthew Henry takes it even further in his commentary on the Scriptures, filling out the essence of David's experience with his God:

> He knew something of the beauty of the Lord, the infinite and transcendent amiableness of the divine being and perfections; His holiness is His beauty (Psalm 110:3), His goodness is His beauty, Zechariah 9:17. The harmony of all His attributes is the beauty of His nature.

I like that. The beauty of the Lord is "the harmony of all His attributes." And David doesn't want a mere glimpse—he wants to "behold," that is, to gaze longingly into the wonder of the Creator.

To simply dwell in the Lord's presence and appreciate His beauty isn't enough, though. David understood that these were things to be considered. Pondered. Meditated on.

Meditate in His temple: Biblical meditation is a wonderful privilege, for it allows us to genuinely focus on our God. Some see David here as meditating on his troubles and how to find escape or resolution to them, and that may be so. But it seems that being in the presence of God and beholding the beauty of the Lord would demand that David's thoughts go to higher ground—to meditating on the worth and wonder of the Lord himself. In a life filled with trials and heartache, it's easy to focus our attention on the troubles that plague us, but when we are aware of God's loving presence and consider His matchless worth, it is hard to meditate on anything else but Him and His greatness—and His sufficiency.

This is where the light of God's person and presence has brought David. This is what he seeks. His one thing. And it would be difficult, if not impossible, to find anything or anyone more worthy of such radically undivided focus.

Stepping Forward

In Psalm 27:7, David will once again turn his attention to the challenges before him, but before doing so he draws an important conclusion born of his time in the light and presence of the Lord: God can be trusted with his life. David's confidence is well-placed, for he rightly understands that the capabilities of his God surpass any threat he might face. The peace that springs from the light that has penetrated his darkness leads David to confidently declare:

> For on the day of trouble He will conceal me
> in His tabernacle;
> He will hide me in the secret place of His tent;
> He will lift me up on a rock.
> And now my head will be lifted up above my
> enemies around me,

> and I will offer sacrifices in His tent with
> shouts of joy;
> I will sing, yes, I will sing praises to the Lord.
> (vv. 5–6)

Of David's commitment to worship in verse 6, *The Expositor's Bible Commentary* says:

> When God protects his own by setting them safely as on a high rock, his people have reason to rejoice. Rejoicing casts out fear. Confident of God's help in trouble, the psalmist anticipates a victory over the enemies who have troubled God's people (cf. vv. 2–3). . . . His expressions of loyalty result from a trusting heart. He knows that he cannot buy God off with his offerings. He knows that his covenantal God cares for his own. Weiser comments, "We are here confronted with a truly living communion with God, with a mutual receiving and giving."

We need to ask ourselves: What is the defining one thing I desire? Where does it place my heart? A truly living communion with God is a one thing worthy of our best desires. And that one thing is the desire we will spend eternity exploring—never to be disappointed and never to be tired of Him, His beauty, and His light. For He himself is the ultimate one thing.

As followers of Christ, this one thing draws us deeply to the Christ who gave His all for us, that we might say with songwriter William R. Featherstone,

> My Jesus, I love Thee, I know Thou art mine;
> For Thee all the follies of sin I resign;
> My gracious Redeemer, my Savior art Thou;

If ever I loved Thee, my Jesus, 'tis now.

I love Thee because Thou has first loved me
And purchased my pardon on Calvary's tree;
I love Thee for wearing the thorns on Thy
brow;
If ever I loved Thee, my Jesus, 'tis now.

I'll love Thee in life, I will love Thee in death,
And praise Thee as long as Thou lendest me
breath,
And say when the death dew lies cold on my
brow:
If ever I loved Thee, my Jesus, 'tis now.

Questions for Personal Reflection or Group Discussion

1. What are the desires of your heart? What desires are positive and appropriate, and what desires are destructive and unwise? What is the root of those desires, whether good or bad?
2. Consider again the quote from St. Augustine, "You have made us for yourself, O Lord, and our hearts are restless until they rest in you." What are some things people desire, hoping that in them they will find rest? Which have you longed for, and what was the result of that longing?
3. It is important that we do not overly idealize David. Though a man after God's heart, he was a flawed, fallen human being, just like we are—not a super saint carved from marble. How does this help us to

identify better with David's struggles? How could it cause us to be concerned about our own capacity for unwise choices?

4. What are some practical ways that we can "dwell in the house of the Lord"? How does that dwelling compare to the branch abiding in the vine (John 15)?
5. How can beholding the beauty of the Lord give a clearer perspective to our troubles and trials? How can His matchless wonder cut our problems down to size?

6

FOCUSING ON A BALANCED THING

It is good that you grasp ***one thing*** while not letting go of the other; for one who fears God comes out with both of them.

Ecclesiastes 7:18

Some things are just crazy. Imagine you are living in New York City on the morning of August 7, 1974. Construction of the twin towers of the World Trade Center is not yet completed, but you can't help but lift your eyes to their peaks as you walk by. Then, to your surprise, you notice what looks like a cable stretched between the two buildings. It is unexpected, but you easily pass it off as some element of the construction project. Until.

As you are gazing up, you see someone actually step out onto that cable. At a height of 1,368 feet! You fear desperately that this person will fall to his death, but you can't stop staring at the scene. Over the course of the next forty-five minutes, the tiny figure overhead crosses between the buildings no less than eight times. At other times he dances, kneels, or even waves to the crowds watching below. Like I said: some things are just crazy.

But for Philippe Petit, the high-wire walker on that summer New York morning, it wasn't a matter of crazy or sane. It was about a carefully trained sense of balance that allowed him to safely complete his demonstration—as he did repeatedly in other places as well.

Balance is a vital thing we see a toddler first experiment with as she takes her first tentative steps. Several years later that child takes it further as she makes her first attempt at riding a bicycle—with the training wheels removed. Skinned knees and crocodile tears accompany the learning experiences in balance until, perhaps, we encounter that same child as a teenager competing in gymnastics in the Olympics. Her apparatus of choice? You guessed it. The balance beam. A piece of leather-wrapped wood that stretches sixteen feet long but is a miniscule 3.9 inches wide. Hence the need for balance.

Balance, or the lack of it, has been a challenge frequently for my wife, Marlene, who periodically experiences bouts of vertigo. More than just the title of an old Alfred Hitchcock movie, vertigo is an actual physical condition often connected to an inner ear imbalance. When vertigo hits, Marlene battles continual dizziness, and she cannot stand without falling over. Balance is lost and the ability to function normally goes with it.

Clearly, balance is a very versatile concept that can speak to both physical and emotional well-being. However, as is often the case, these physical realities have spiritual parallels. The Scriptures frequently speak to issues of balance, sometimes as a picture of integrity in the marketplace.

Balance and Business

The website of one of the premier makers of sports shoes, clothes, and gear says this of its mission:

> At New Balance, our job is to aid athletes in their pursuits, whether that means helping professional athletes set records and win medals, or propelling everyday athletes to achieve a new PR, run their first 5K or just to live a more healthy and active lifestyle.

For New Balance, balance is not just a catchphrase or a buzzword. It is inherent to their mission of making products that help people grow and develop in their fitness and achieve their best. And it's a key element of their history as a business. The company began by producing arch support inserts for shoes to provide both comfort and improved balance for the wearer. Back in 1906, New Balance founder William Riley modeled those inserts after the three prongs of the foot of a chicken—which he said produced perfect balance.

While balance was the core of how that particular company was founded, in a much broader sense balance is foundational to any business that operates with integrity. This was literally true in the marketplaces of the Old Testament. Since most food and precious metals were traded by weight, having scales (balances) that produced true and accurate results was vital. It was far too easy to swindle someone by using intentionally inaccurate weights on the scales. This issue of integrity in business was at the core of statements in both the Torah and the Wisdom Literature of the Old Testament:

> You shall have accurate balances, accurate weights, an accurate ephah, and an accurate hin; I am the LORD your God, who brought you out from the land of Egypt. (Leviticus 19:36)

> A just balance and scales belong to the LORD; All the weights of the bag are His concern. (Proverbs 16:11)

Not only were just balances an issue in business but they were also an issue in Israel's religious laws. This should be no surprise, for how we operate a business is an expression of who we are and what we value. Just balances reveal a heart committed to integrity.

Balance in Attitude

There are millions of web pages that promote living a balanced life or having a balanced personality. The problem with those sites is that many of them contradict each other pretty dramatically regarding how to achieve such balance! In fact, how you define being balanced may be totally dependent upon the value system you embrace.

In Proverbs 30:8–9 we read:

> Keep deception and lies far from me,
> Give me neither poverty nor riches;

> Feed me with the food that is my portion,
> So that I will not be full and deny You and
> say, "Who is the LORD?"
> And that I will not become impoverished and
> steal,
> And profane the name of my God.

This thought is fundamentally the same idea Jesus lifted up when He taught us to pray, "Give us this day our daily bread," or literally, "bread for the day" (Matthew 6:11). In this proverb, the ancient sage Agur cries out for the need for balance—because lack of balance has consequences both in how we view life and in how we view, or even relate to, God. Yet how can we discover the kind of balance that is so needed in a world filled with the wild pendular mood swings of the mob or the urgency of the moment?

To get insight that is beyond ourselves on this (or any other) issue, it is helpful to see what the Bible has to say—for there we find the timeless wisdom of our wise God. To that end, we should remember that, for the most part, the Scriptures fall into two big categories—texts that are descriptive and texts that are prescriptive. A *descriptive* text is not one that is telling us what right living or right thinking looks like. It is there to tell us, in a true and honest way, what happened. For example, when Scripture tells us that the Old Testament patriarch Jacob had multiple wives, it is not endorsing polygamy. It is giving us an inspired, accurate account of what happened.

At other times the wisdom of Scripture takes the form of something *prescriptive*, that is, an inspired challenge or encouragement telling us how we can engage life in a balanced way. For example, the King James Version of Philippians 4:5 reads, "Let your moderation be known unto all men. The Lord is at hand."

What is that saying? Modern translations, such as the New American Standard Bible, give us a hint by translating the same verse this way: "Let your gentle spirit be known to all people. The Lord is near."

What does moderation have to do with a gentle spirit? The website Bible or Not says:

> *Moderation* is the opposite of *excess*, and the Bible clearly teaches that we should be known for our moderation—it doesn't explicitly say *moderation in all things*, but it does say that our very nature should be marked by moderation. So if our moderation is to be known unto everyone, that could not be accomplished if we were moderate in only a few things. What is interesting though, when Paul writes about *excess*, he cautions about excess of wine (i.e. gluttony) but he says we should be filled with the Spirit implying you could never have excess of that.

Moderation seems to point toward a balanced approach to life that avoids the extremes—finding good ground in the balance. This especially applies in how we view others. This word translated as "moderation" or "gentle spirit" in Philippians 4:5 speaks directly to that concern, as *The Expositor's Bible Commentary* explains:

> "Gentleness" puts up with other people's faults and when provoked will not seek revenge. It is a spirit that is open, conciliatory, and trusting of one's neighbor . . . and it is the opposite of being contentious and self-seeking.

This moderate, gentle spirit avoids the extremes in human relationships. Building on the theme of joy (v. 4), which is internal and personal, Paul now turns the focus of his letter to what is external and relational. *The Bible Knowledge Commentary* says that this balanced approach to others, characterized by this gentleness,

> Suggests a forebearing, nonretaliatory spirit. Joy, an inner quality in relation to circumstances, may not always be seen; but the way one reacts to others—whether in gentleness or harshness—will be noticed.

If you look back just a few verses, you'll see that Philippians 4 opens with a challenge to Euodia and Syntyche, two women in the congregation at Philippi who were in conflict. Not only was the conflict affecting their relationship with each other but it was also impacting the life of the church. So severe was this impact that Paul calls on a trusted coworker at Philippi ("true companion"; v. 3) to intercede and attempt to bring reconciliation. That is where balance is most clearly seen. Reconciliation is all about making things right and restoring what has been broken. Reconciliation seeks to bring what is off-kilter back into proper balance.

What is involved in having such a balanced attitude toward others? In Romans 12, after building a theological platform for a life rooted in God's grace in Romans 1–11, Paul unveils the kinds of actions and attitudes that reveal a balanced heart:

> Love must be free of hypocrisy. Detest what is evil; cling to what is good. Be devoted to one another in brotherly love;

> give preference to one another in honor; not lagging behind in diligence, fervent in spirit, serving the Lord; rejoicing in hope, persevering in tribulation, devoted to prayer, contributing to the needs of the saints, practicing hospitality.
>
> Bless those who persecute you; bless and do not curse. Rejoice with those who rejoice, and weep with those who weep. Be of the same mind toward one another; do not be haughty in mind, but associate with the lowly. Do not be wise in your own estimation. Never repay evil for evil to anyone. Respect what is right in the sight of all people. If possible, so far as it depends on you, be at peace with all people. (vv. 9–18)

All of that wise counsel fairly screams of a life lived in balance. Free of hypocrisy. One another. Hope versus trial. Rejoice and weep. All of the ideas Paul presents seem to grow out of the good ground of a heart that has been reconciled to God and are lived out with regard to one another—perhaps captured best by verse 18: "If possible, so far as it depends on you, be at peace with all people."

That sounds precisely like the moderation or gentle spirit Paul was encouraging in Philippians 4:5. One of the most revealing characteristics of a life lived in balance is manifested in how we respond to one another. When we are not living such a life, we end up in conflict (like Euodia and Syntyche of Philippians 4). However, when the moderating gentleness of a balanced life is in view, the lovely, inspiring qualities of Romans 12 reveal both a heart changed by grace and a life fueled and empowered by the Holy Spirit. After all, the fruit of the Spirit (Galatians 5:22–23) is the internal fuel that drives the external attitudes of a balanced life.

Not surprisingly, Jesus himself stands as the supreme example of balance—both in attitude and in spirit. In the prologue to John's gospel, the apostle affirms this truth in the second half of a verse whose first half we considered in an earlier chapter. In John 1:14 we read,

> And the Word became flesh, and dwelt among us; and we saw His glory, glory as of the only Son from the Father, full of grace and truth.

Notice that He came full of both grace and truth. These two ideas are not mutually exclusive, but they do operate on opposite ends of the spectrum—and if either is overemphasized, it does harm to the other. If we become so much about grace that we set aside God's truth found in Scripture, we harm the truth. If we push truth and its apparent demands too hard, we lose the grace and compassion that help us embrace one another as people in need. Jesus came full of both—perfect balance in two of the most critical elements of living the life of faith. In fact, I am convinced that this is the essence of true justice, equity, and fairness. True justice is found in Jesus, for in Him is the perfect balance of merciful grace and necessary truth.

Likewise, we see Jesus's balance of spirit—what Paul called a "gentle spirit"—in Jesus's most self-defining statement. In Matthew 11:29, Jesus says, "Take My yoke upon you and learn from Me, for I am gentle and humble in heart, and you will find rest for your souls."

Though He is the Creator of the universe and God in human flesh, Jesus displays himself as gentle. As we see His balance in character (grace and truth), He deals with people with a heart of gentleness—perfectly modeling Paul's call to moderation and balance in Philippians 4:5.

Balance in Living

This brings us to where balance intersects with this chapter's one thing, and it is found in the book of Ecclesiastes—one of the more challenging books in the Old Testament.

Attributed to Solomon by many scholars, Ecclesiastes allows us to hear David's son expressing the despair of living in a world that is out of balance. *The New Bible Commentary* describes Ecclesiastes this way:

> What then is the purpose and abiding message of Ecclesiastes? It is a reply to the unrelieved pessimism of much ancient thought. Yet at the same time it does not envisage a superficial "faith" which does not take adequate account of the fallenness of the world.

Notice the balancing elements of that statement. Ecclesiastes seeks to find reasons for hope while not ignoring the sad realities of this world as it really is. That need for balance makes an appearance in the midst of the poet's musings about the highs and lows of life—and it brings us our final one thing.

> Do not be excessively righteous, and do not be overly wise. Why should you ruin yourself? Do not be excessively wicked, and do not be foolish. Why should you die before your time? It is good that you grasp **one thing** while not letting go of the other; for one who fears God comes out with both of them. (7:16–18)

Notice how the New International Version translates verse 18: "It is good to grasp the one and not let go of the other. Whoever fears God will avoid all extremes."

That is exactly what we have been looking at—balance, moderation. Grasping one thing but not letting go of the other. Avoiding all extremes. Of that, *The Bible Knowledge Commentary* gives the historic view of these verses:

> These verses have generally been interpreted as teaching the "golden mean" or a moderate lifestyle, avoiding both overzealous righteousness and overindulgent sinfulness. And righteousness here is generally interpreted as referring to legalistic or Pharisaic self-righteousness.

In *Be Satisfied*, Warren Wiersbe adds:

> Verse 18 balances the warning: we should take hold of true righteousness and should not withdraw from true wisdom, and the way to do it is to walk in the fear of God. "The fear of the Lord is the beginning of wisdom" (Proverbs 9:10) and Jesus Christ is to the believer "wisdom and righteousness" (1 Corinthians 1:30), so God's people need not "manufacture" these blessings themselves.

All of this speaks to why this chapter comes at the end of this book. We have been looking at various one things and talking about avoiding distraction by keeping our focus in the right places. All of that is true. All of that is important.

And all of that can be abused.

It is far too easy for us to allow focus to turn into obsession. As a wise Bible teacher once said in my hearing, "Any truth taken to an extreme becomes a form of heresy." So we find the wisdom of balance in both theology and life:

- Jesus is God, yet Jesus is human.
- God is sovereign, yet people have free will.
- Salvation is by faith, yet salvation is made visible in works.
- The child of God is in the world, yet the child of God is not of the world.

The list could go on and on, but the point is this: we need to rely on the wisdom of God in every situation of life so we can live out that wisdom in balance with the world of which we are a part. If it is possible to abuse Scripture by taking it to extremes, it is likewise possible to abuse the one things we have been considering together. This provides yet another call to balance. So how does balance inform our one things?

- The value of giving away all we have is balanced by being wise stewards of all that God has entrusted to us.
- The innocence of saying "this one thing I know" is balanced by the call to grow, learn, and move forward in our understanding of our God and His Son.
- The longing to pursue relationship with God is balanced by the understanding that apart from Christ and His grace such a pursuit is impossible.
- The one thing of meditation and quiet learning in the presence of Jesus is balanced by rightly motivated service of one another.

- The longing to dwell in God's house and presence is balanced by the challenge to be salt and light in a world that desperately needs both.

However, avoiding all extremes is not a call to a bland, vanilla, middle-of-the-road faith. It is much more. It is a call to live within the wisdom of a God who is more than capable of navigating us through the pitfalls and problems that living in a world of extremes—and distractions—can create. My favorite hymn, "Be Thou My Vision," reminds me to pray:

> Be Thou my wisdom, and Thou my true
> Word;
> I ever with Thee and Thou with me, Lord;
> Thou my great Father and I, Thy true son;
> Thou in me dwelling, and I with Thee one.

Only in reliance on God's perfect wisdom can we rightly pursue the one things the Scriptures set before us, while maintaining the balance to do so in a way that not only honors Him but also protects us from the dangers of excess—even in the most important things of life.

Questions for Personal Reflection or Group Discussion

1. Why is a balanced life so difficult to achieve? What are some areas where you struggle with maintaining a sense of balance?
2. How does balance speak to the issue of integrity in the Old Testament? How does balance represent gentleness of spirit in the New Testament?

3. Considering the one things we looked at in chapters 1 through 5, which might be the easiest for you to keep in balance? Why?
4. Considering the one things we looked at in chapters 1 through 5, which might be the hardest for you to keep in balance? Why?
5. Read through the exhortations of Romans 12:9–18. How do they express a life balanced in the wisdom of God? How could that balance be seen in your relationships with others?

CONCLUSION

ONE LAST THING

We have been considering one things—things that can help us to find focus in a world of distractions. It is my sincere hope that these have been helpful, providing some practical handholds for navigating our way through a challenging life in a difficult world. However, if none of these one things had been articulated in the Scriptures, we could still find the CliffsNotes version of their challenge for focus in Hebrews 12:1–2, where we read:

> Therefore, since we also have such a great cloud of witnesses surrounding us, let's rid ourselves of every obstacle and the sin which so easily entangles us, and let's run with endurance the race that is set before us, looking only at Jesus, the originator and perfecter of the faith, who for the joy set before Him endured the cross, despising the shame, and has sat down at the right hand of the throne of God.

As we learn to place our focus where it is best placed—on our Lord and His great love and grace for us—we find the ultimate example and role model. We find someone who is worthy of our most intense focus. We find reason for what Oswald Chambers called "my utmost for His highest."

And we discover more. We discover that our focus on Christ flows from His absolute and unflinching focus on the cross. Twice in Luke 9 (vv. 51, 53), as Jesus began His journey to Jerusalem and the cross that awaited Him there, Luke says that Jesus "set His face to go to Jerusalem" (NKJV).

We fix our eyes on the One who "set His face" to go to Jerusalem and die on the cross on our behalf. In the midst of all that we may encounter in this world, this rises above the rest—Jesus is the ultimate object of our attention, of our hearts, and of our aspirations. He is the ultimate one thing that draws us home. Focus on Him.

Also by Bill Crowder

Available for God's Purpose
Before Christmas
For This He Came
God of Surprise
Let's Talk
Living with Courage
Moving Beyond Failure
My Hope Is in You
Overcoming Life's Challenges
Seeing the Heart of Christ
The Spotlight of Faith
Trusting God in Hard Times
Windows on Christmas
Windows on Easter

Devotionals

A Compassionate Heart
A Deep Dependence

Help us get the word out!

Our Daily Bread Publishing exists to feed the soul with the Word of God.

If you appreciated this book, please let others know.

- Pick up another copy to give as a gift.
- Share a link to the book or mention it on social media.
- Write a review on your blog, on a book-seller's website, or at our own site (odb.org/store)
- Recommend this book for your church, book club, or small group.

Connect with us:

@ourdailybread

@ourdailybread

@ourdailybread

Our Daily Bread Publishing
PO Box 3566
Grand Rapids, Michigan 49501 USA

books@odb.org